Industry
and
Transport
in
Scottish
Museums

The 'Craigievar Express' steam car outside Craigievar Castle. The vehicle is now in the Grampian Transport Museum, Alford, Aberdeenshire. (see p.60)

Industry
and
Transport
in
Scottish
Museums

J. R. HUME & J. D. STORER

The Stationery Office Limited
South Gyle Crescent, Edinburgh EH12 9EB

First published 1997

Applications for reproduction should be made to
The Stationery Office Limited

British Cataloguing in Publication Data

A catalogue record for this book is available from the British Library

ISBN 0 11 495256 6

Dedication

To all those who care for the buildings and
artefacts included in this book

CONTENTS

The A-frame headgear at Barony Colliery, Ayrshire, before demolition of surrounding buildings. (see p.21)

ACKNOWLEDGEMENTS

The authors would like to thank all those in museums and elsewhere who helped in the preparation of this book, and especially those who provided illustrations and agreed to their reproduction. Unless otherwise stated, the illustrations were provided by the museums concerned, and are their copyright. The illustrations of the National Museums of Scotland (Chambers Street, Museum of Flight and Scottish Agricultural Museum) are also Crown Copyright, as is the photograph of the retort house at Biggar, which was kindly supplied by Historic Scotland. They are also grateful to the staff of The Stationery Office Limited for their patience. The book has been prepared over a long period, and the authors would be grateful for information updating the entries, which have been kept as up to date as possible.

In the task of producing the text the authors are grateful for assistance with the typing and checking to Mrs S A Storer.

List of photographs supplied by John R. Hume: **Prelims**, vi, 1, 4, 8, 12 and 14.

List of Museums, 16 (both), 17, 18 (lower), 20, 21, 22, (both), 23 (upper), 25, 26, 27, 29 (lower), 30, 31 (both), 32, 33 (both), 35 (both), 36, 37, 38, 39 (both), 40, 41 (both), 43, 45 (lower), 47, 48, 51, 52, 54 (upper), 56, 57, 58 (both), 59, 63, 64 (both), 65, 68, 69, 70, 71, 72 (both), 74 (both), 75 (both), 78, 79, 80, 86, 87, 89, 92, 93, 94, 95, 96 (right), 97, 100 (both), 102 (both), 103, 104, 107 (both), 110, 111 (both), 112 (lower), 113, 114, 115 (both), 119, 120, 121, 123 (lower), 124 (upper), 126, 127, 128 and 130.

J. R. Hume

J. D. Storer

LIST OF MUSEUMS AND SITES

INTRODUCTION

SCOTLAND'S INDUSTRIAL HISTORY IN SITES AND MUSEUMS

That Scotland's industrial and transport history is of unusual interest has only been recognized comparatively recently. The whole spectrum of industrial activity, from craft trades to the heaviest of heavy industry has been represented in Scotland, and though changing economic patterns have inevitably extinguished many once important activities, what remains is still interesting, often grand, and always stimulating. For the 'romance of industry' is still, for those who explore it, singularly fascinating. How men and women have devised ways of making things that are wanted or needed for civilized life (indeed life of any kind), how these ways have been operated, the personalities and the communities which have shaped and been shaped by industrial enterprise, how people and goods have been moved from place to place: all these are central to an understanding not just of Scotland, but of the world as we know it. This book points the reader to where he or she can find out more about Scotland's industrial past and her transport systems and thus enter a world of human endeavour of fundamental interest and importance.

The museums and sites included in this volume represent only a small part of all the surviving physical evidence of Scotland's industrial and transport history. All the more obviously important museums and accessible preserved sites are listed, together with many smaller locations. Because it is impossible to be absolutely comprehensive some will have been left out. We hope that no-one will take offence at that, and we will be glad to receive details of omissions. Equally, some museums and sites may have changed since the respective accounts were put together. The general pattern of the book is that entries are arranged alphabetically by name or place and indexed under name, place and region, for convenient reference by tourists and day visitors. This introduction is thematic, and because many museums have collections and displays relating to more than one industrial activity they will appear more than once.

Weaver's cottage, Kilbarchan, Renfrewshire. (see p.69)

RURAL INDUSTRIES

The most universal and basic of industries are those in which food is processed. Grain has been mechanically ground since Roman times, and two types of watermill were in use from that period. The smaller and simpler is the horizontal, or norse mill, with its wheel paddles set in a horizontal plane, the wheel axle driving a pair of millstones directly. This type, apparently once widespread in Scotland, was by the late 19th century confined to the north and north-west mainland, the outer isles, Orkney and Shetland. The sole surviving Orkney horizontal mill, the Click Mill at Dounby, is in State care, and there are actively preserved or restored examples in Lewis (Shawbost), and Shetland (Southvoe). A relocated mill in the Highland Folk Life Museum in Kingussie is untypical. The Scottish Agricultural Museum at Ingliston has a collection of pieces of horizontal mill.

Horizontal mills could only grind enough grain for at most a handful of families, and the more powerful vertical, or Vitruvian mill became the standard type in most parts of Scotland. Their remains, often converted to other uses, may still be found in considerable numbers, and a reasonably representative sample has been actively preserved. The oldest is probably Preston Mill, East Linton (parts of which may be from as early as the 17th century), now the property of The National Trust for Scotland, which also owns Barry Mill. Historic Scotland looks after New Abbey Mill, with its unorthodox machinery and layout, and Tormiston Mill, the interior of which is now mainly a visitor centre. Tormiston is a good example of a large, developed water-powered mill of the late 19th century. There are other country mills open to visitors at Blair Atholl, Sandhead and Elgin, and there may well be more. Sandhead and Elgin are in the care of their local district councils. Of the larger town mills only one is currently accessible to the public. This is the Lower City Mills at Perth, which operated commercially until the 1960s, and which is now run by Perth and Kinross District Council.

Of the other major grain-using industries, brewing and distilling are very unevenly represented. There are three 'traditional' breweries working in Scotland – Belhaven (Dunbar), Caledonian (Edinburgh) and Maclays (Alloa) – but none is preserved as such, though it may be possible to arrange visits. The distilling industry, on the other hand, is very publicity conscious, and most malt whisky distilleries allow visits. Some have elaborate visitor facilities, most of them on the Whisky Heritage Trail in the north east. These are all worth seeing, especially for the distillery tours, but the carefully contrived visitor facilities are rarely authentic, though usually admirably constructed. Three distilleries are mentioned in the text for their unusual historical interest. Dallas Dhu Distillery, near Forres, is in the care of Historic Scotland, and its fabric is carefully maintained in the condition in which it was when closed in 1983. Glenkinchie Distillery, an unorthodox Lowland distillery built in brick, houses the United Distillers' collection of distillery equipment, a very important one, preserving many of the implements rendered obsolete by technical developments in the industry since the 1950s. Of the 'visitor distilleries', Edradour has been included for the insights it gives into the early history of malt whisky distilling. The external appearance of the buildings has been carefully conserved, though the interior has unfortunately been somewhat modified in the interests of access and safety. Apart from these sites, several local museums hold material relating to distilling, especially illicit distilling.

The handcraft textile industries, once widespread, are now reduced to the status of curiosities. The National Trust for Scotland's weaver's cottage in Kilbarchan is a large and elaborate building for its date, and probably housed a clothier's household. There is also a weaver's cottage, treated as a museum, in Airdrie. Handlooms, such as would have been used in the homes of weavers, exist in a number of museums, including Dunfermline, Paisley and the visitor centre at Cathcartston,

Dalmellington. Some of these are plain looms, used for simple weaves, but there are pattern looms in Dunfermline and Paisley. The products of hand-loom weaving may be found in many local museums; an outstanding collection is in Paisley, dominated by the famous shawls, but also including samples of fancy muslins, which were made in quantity in the west of Scotland. Though not 'officially' preserved, handloom weavers' cottages survive in numbers in Kilbarchan, Crosshill (near Maybole), Darvel and Dairsie, to name just a few of the many towns and villages in which the weaving trade was the dominant one.

Rural textile manufacture was often controlled by city merchants, and the produce destined for export, or for sale in urban markets. Ironworking in the countryside was, however, generally for local purposes – horse-shoeing, repair of, or constructing agricultural implements, and making such simple ironwork as door and gate hinges and latches. There were semi-urban places like parts of Falkirk and St Ninian's parish near Stirling, where nailmaking was practised in a manner similar to weaving, but generally smiddies were small, individual units serving fairly large areas. Many of them survive as buildings, some long disused, others converted to other purposes, and a few still working. Very few have been preserved, and are accessible to the public. The Isle of Arran Museum at Brodick incorporates a smiddy complete with all its equipment, and at The National Trust for Scotland's smiddy at Kippen one can still see the traditional craft being practised.

Rural joiners worked in a similar way to blacksmiths, generally serving local needs, making doors, windows, gates, simple furniture – and coffins, for they were often undertakers too. Many joinery shops survive in use, for there remains a need in rural areas for repair and refitting joinery and, of course, for undertaking. Only one joiner's shop is currently open to the public, at Fordyce in Banffshire. Joiners' tools are, however, part of the stock in trade in most museums, as are the hand tools used by coopers in making and repairing barrels. Coopering was, despite the similarity in tools and technique, generally organised in connection with breweries or distillers. One of the Speyside cooperages offers tours to visitors. Glenkinchie Distillery museum has a particularly fine collection of tools, and there is a recreation of a cooper's workshop at Dallas Dhu.

MINING AND QUARRYING

Coal, ironstone and oil shale were economically by far the most important minerals mined in Scotland, but because ironstone mining ceased during the interwar years this industry is only represented in museums by mineral samples. The coal mining industry was one of Scotland's most important, and it is not surprising that it looms large in museum and site preservation. The premier museum is the Scottish Mining Museum. Its two sites, Prestongrange and Newtongrange, are now separately managed, a situation reflecting their origins. Prestongrange, the site of a colliery, brick and pipe works, was built up round Scotland's only surviving Cornish pumping engine, which was spared when the colliery site was cleared. At Newtongrange, it was the great steam winding engine of the Lady Victoria Colliery, a showpiece of the 1890s, which was the focus. There, it is the completeness of the survival which is of the utmost significance. Other colliery sites with survivals of interest are the Mary Pit, Lochore, Highhouse Colliery, and Barony Colliery, the latter two at Auchinleck. There are also displays of artifacts associated with coal mining in many museums, the most important at the Royal Museum of Scotland in Chambers Street, Edinburgh and Summerlee, where there is a simulated underground experience, and where the only rotative Newcomen engine in Britain has been re-erected. The mining and processing of oil shale has its own museum at Livingston, with a re-created mining gallery and displays on shale oil extraction and refining.

Clay mine, Birkhill, West Lothian. (see p.25)

The transport systems associated with coal and oil shale mining are widely represented in museum collections, especially by steam locomotives in the Scottish Railway Preservation Society and Ayrshire Railway Preservation Group collections. Livingston Oil Museum has an electric locomotive from the Oakbank Oil Company's narrow-gauge system, and at Dunaskin there are mine cars and an underground battery locomotive.

Other mining industries which have attracted museum attention are lead extraction in Leadhills and Wanlockhead and clay mining at Birkhill, Bo'ness. The museum at Wanlockhead houses models of mine pumps, simulation of a mineral vein, and of a lead smelter. Mineral specimens from the mines also feature. Visitors may also tour a lead mine adit, and view a row of cottages fitted out to show miners' living conditions at different periods. The sites of Pate's Knowe's lead smelter and of the Bay Mine may also be seen. Historic Scotland have in care a unique water-balance pumping engine, a working model of which may be seen in the museum. In both Wanlockhead and Leadhills there are miners' libraries. The Leadhills one is open to the public, and contains the 'bargain books' in which miners' contracts for work were recorded. At Birkhill visitors can go underground to view the extensive 'stoop and room' workings for refractory fireclay.

The quarrying of building stones was one of Scotland's most widely dispersed industries, and some quarries were spectacularly large, notably Rubishaw granite quarry in Aberdeen and Craigleith sandstone quarry in Edinburgh. So far as museum and on-site preservation are concerned, however, with one exception it is the small and medium-sized enterprises that have been marked. At Locharbriggs, near Dumfries, a crane has been preserved at the entrance to the still-active quarry. The Caithness flagstone quarry at Castlehill is the centrepiece of a visitor centre (not yet open), and slate quarrying features in the North Lorn Folk Museum in Glencoe Village, in the Easdale Island museum and in a visitor centre at Ballachulish.

PRIMARY PROCESSING

Immediately linked to quarrying is the burning of lime. This was a very significant industry in the 18th and 19th centuries, when lime was very widely used to sweeten the natural acid soils of Lowland Scotland, as well as in building. Limekilns survive throughout the country in varying stages of decay. A few are actively preserved. At Catcraigs, near Dunbar, a range of kilns was restored in the 1960s and these are in the care of East Lothian District Council. Not far away, Scottish Nuclear has restored a kiln near Torness Power Station. There is also a good range of three kilns at Park, near Closeburn, Dumfriesshire. Most spectacular of all is the great kiln complex at Charlestown, on the Forth estuary. It was built up by successive Earls of Elgin, and the estate has active plans for full consolidation and restoration. In the meantime, the kilns may be viewed from the road, as can the harbour built for the shipment of coal and lime.

Salt boiling – the extraction of salt from seawater by evaporation in heated pans – was a distinctive Scottish industry from the 17th century. Though its main centre was the Forth estuary, there were also several works on the Clyde, and others scattered along Scotland's coastline. The industry flourished because of preferential taxation until the 1820s, when the removal of duties led to its almost complete collapse. Two saltworks are being preserved and will be accessible to visitors. Both are in Fife. At St Monans, the windmill used to pump seawater to the pans has been consolidated and fitted with a viewing gallery, and the salt-pan complex partly excavated. At Preston Island, which is not currently accessible to the public, but which is visible from Valleyfield, the remains are more complete, and include three salt-pan buildings as well as the pumping engine house for the associated coal pit.

Of the other primary processing industries dependent on mineral extraction the most economically important was iron smelting. Three ironwork sites are actively preserved. Of these, the oldest and the most complete is Bonawe Ironworks at Taynuilt, which was founded in 1753 by English ironmasters from the Furness area. It used charcoal as a fuel, and is the most intact survivor of its type in Britain. At Glen Nant and Dalavich, the Forestry Commission has laid out trails through woodland that supplied Bonawe with fuel. These trails take in charcoal-burning platforms. Another charcoal-fuelled blast furnace at Furnace, Loch Fyne, may be viewed from the road. Of the economically much more important coal-fuelled Lowland ironworks, two sites are now in museum complexes. At Summerlee the remains of part of the ironworks have been excavated, revealing the lower courses of blowing engine houses, associated boiler settings, and blast furnaces and their linked hot-blast stoves. The slightly later works at Waterside, near Dalmellington, is now part of the open-air museum there. Here the furnace bank, blowing engine house, workshops and offices all survive, and have been restored. The site of the blast furnaces would probably repay excavation. Both Summerlee and Dalmellington give a hint of the scale of Victorian ironworks, and at Dalmellington the works itself can still be seen in the context of the mineral railways, ironstone and coal pits, workers' housing and community buildings called into being to serve it. Though no complete post-charcoal blast furnaces survive (apart from the three at Ravenscraig, not yet dismantled at the time of writing) there is a fine model in the Royal Museum of Scotland of a furnace and stove as used at Glengarnock Ironworks.

This is a convenient point to include the ceramics industry, for in Scotland it drew its raw materials from the coal measures, and some of its products were used to line the blast furnaces and limekilns, and to pack the hot blast stoves mentioned above. The links are reinforced by the setting of the surviving preserved brick kilns. One of these is at Prestongrange, next to the colliery site. The other two are at Dalmellington, where they replaced the blast furnaces and by-product recovery plant. The kiln at Prestongrange, and one of those at Dalmellington, are of the standard longitudinally-arched Hoffman continuous type. The other Dalmellington kiln has separate transverse-arched chambers, and was used for making engineering bricks, which were fired at a higher temperature than common building bricks. There is a good brick collection at Summerlee, and in both Summerlee and the Falkirk Museums' workshops there are items of equipment from the local ceramics industries. The Birkhill clay mine has already been mentioned. The bottle kilns used in pottery-making until recent years are now only represented by the two kilns at Portobello which survived the demolition of Buchan's pottery when the firm moved to Crieff (where the modern pottery welcomes visitors). Locally-made pottery features in many museum collections, notably in Kirkcaldy, Bo'ness, the People's Palace in Glasgow, the Huntly House Museum in Edinburgh, and in the McLean Museum, Greenock. Scottish glass also features in many museum collections, but the only substantial reminder of this industry is the surviving glass cone in Alloa, which may be viewed from the road. The scale of the modern glass-bottle trade can be judged by the extent to which the cone, itself a very substantial structure, is dwarfed by the United Glass plant.

TEXTILES

The large-scale manufacturing industries of which brick, pottery and glass making may be said to be examples, are more clearly identified with textile manufacturing, engineering and shipbuilding, all trades in which Scotland has been (and in some instances still is) notable. The handcraft textile industries have already been mentioned, and some of these persisted long after factory production developed. In the Outer Isles some tweed is still woven on foot-powered looms housed in the homes of the workers, but apart from these and self-consciously craft producers the factory system has long since triumphed. The cotton industry was the first to be mechanised, largely because of the shortness and relative uniformity of the fibres being processed. The first cotton-spinning mills in Scotland were built in the 1770s and 80s. Part of a mill built in 1780 may be seen from the street in Johnstone, but a much more impressive monument to early cotton spinning survives in New Lanark, where No. 1 Mill (now rebuilt to its original height), and the rear wall of No. 2 Mill, survive from the 1780s, together with most of the original housing. Though the complex was subsequently modified, overall it gives a very good impression of a large factory village of the first industrial revolution. Remains of other early cotton mills can also be seen at Deanston and Stanley (view from road), and at Blantyre the David Livingstone Centre is housed in two blocks of cotton workers' houses. No authentic early cotton-spinning machinery survives in Scotland. Though cotton spinning in Scotland declined in the later 19th century, this generalisation did not extend to thread manufacture, which expanded hugely after the invention of the sewing machine. It became particularly associated with Paisley, and the museum there houses displays on thread making. Port Glasgow enjoyed a similar special link with rope and net making, both of which are represented in the McLean Museum displays.

The linen trade, which became centred on Dundee and satellite towns, and on Dunfermline, began to be mechanised in the 1790s. As with cotton, it was spinning that was first brought into powered factories. Hand-loom weaving persisted until well into the 19th century. Dundee and Arbroath specialised in heavy textiles, especially sailcloth and bagging. As world trade expanded rapidly from the 1830s, the demand for packaging cloth grew. Dundee merchants, seeking a cheaper material than flax for this range of products, began importing jute from India, and built larger factories to process it. Sailcloth and fine linens, however, continued to be made, and the descendants of these trades are still in being. There are displays on linen and jute textiles in Dundee, Arbroath and Dunfermline museums, the last-named with machinery. Dundee Heritage has acquired a small flax and jute mill, Verdant Works, and is developing it as a museum of the trades which made Dundee a major city. In Blairgowrie, Keathbank Mill, a water-powered jute mill of the 1860s with its original waterwheel and auxiliary steam engine, is now open to the public. Many of the Dundee linen and jute mills have been converted into housing, but remain largely unaltered externally.

Though less significant in the industrial revolution than cotton or linen, the Scottish woollen industry has proved durable and successful, and Scottish woollen garments have a world-wide reputation. The industry was widespread, and there were small country mills in many parts of Scotland. Those at Knockando on Speyside and Bridgend on Islay, both with antique spinning machinery, are typical in scale. Both operate commercially, though in each case the old machinery can be viewed. In the later 19th century, large-scale woollen manufacture became the speciality of the Border towns (notably Galashiels, Hawick, Selkirk and Langholm), of Dumfries, and of the Clackmannan and Stirling districts. In all these places one can see mill buildings of the period. Of these, three may be singled out. Nether Mill, Galashiels, a multiperiod spinning and weaving mill, is still at work, but offers tours and a museum display; the Mill Trail Visitor Centre in Glentana Mill, Alva, with some typical looms; and at Dangerfield Mill, Hawick, the original carding and spinning machinery survives *in situ* and there are active plans to preserve it. In addition to these, in part of the former Ballantines' Mill at Walkerburn there is the Scottish Museum of Wool Textiles, which is a series of small displays linked to a shop. Two other sites should be mentioned. One is the Hawick Museum at Wilton Lodge, which has a fine collection of knitting machinery, as befits the centre of the hosiery trade. The other is New Lanark, where woollen carding and spinning machinery has been installed to show visitors basic textile processes.

ENGINEERING AND SHIPBUILDING

The engineering industries in Scotland, as elsewhere, grew out of millwrighting, the construction of mill machinery and power transmission. Other influences were boilermaking and clockmaking. From relatively small beginnings in the 17th and 18th centuries, engineering became one of the most characteristic of Scottish industries. The Scots marine engineer, celebrated by Rudyard Kipling in McAndrew's Hymn, was one of the best-known symbols of this, reflecting Scotland's lead from the 1810s to 1914 in marine engineering. Textile machinery, railway locomotives and rolling stock, mining machinery for use both above and below ground, sugar, rice and nut-processing machinery, machine tools (especially for shipbuilding and structural engineering), metal piers, bridges and the like, gas, hydraulic and electrical machinery were all Scottish specialities, and in some of these, notably sugar machinery and shipbuilding machine tools, Scotland unquestionably led the world. Since the 1960s there has been a significant decline in engineering activity in Scotland, but there are still some distinguished firms active in this area.

The engineering industries (loosely interpreted to include ironfounding and other peripheral trades) are fairly well represented both in museum collections and by sites. Products of Scottish engineering feature in collections included here for their transport or other (for example distilling and mining) interests. Among the railway vehicle collections, for instance, there are examples of the work of most of the major, and many minor, Scottish locomotive builders. Scottish-built motor cars and commercial vehicles are also to be found in a number of collections, notably that of the Glasgow Museum of Transport. Sewing machines made in Scotland are in many local museums,

S V Carrick *at the Scottish Maritime Museum, Irvine, Ayrshire. (see p.111)*

and Clydebank Museum has the definitive collection. Scottish-made agricultural machinery may be found in agricultural museums, and products of Scottish ironfounding in, for example, Falkirk Museum's collection. Individual machines are also preserved at some sites, including Hopeman and Locharbriggs (cranes), Port Glasgow (steam hammer), and Dumbarton and Renfrew (marine engines).

The industries that created these objects are much less well represented. Until the Scottish Society for the Preservation of Historical Machinery (SSPHM) was founded in 1971 hardly any machine tools had been preserved in Scotland, in sharp contrast to prime movers, both mobile and stationary. Nor had ironfounding equipment. Though the SSPHM has long ceased to exist, its collections, and others stimulated by its activities, contain representative examples of most of the machine-tool types used in 'traditional' mechanical engineering, and products from many Scottish machine-tool manufacturers. These include not only precision tools, such as lathes, drilling and planing machines, but also the plate and section working tools used in boilermaking, shipbuilding and structural iron and steel working. The biggest displays of machine tools are in Summerlee, but Falkirk Museums and the Scottish Maritime Museum have significant collections, and the National Museums of Scotland have a few. The only engineering works preserved as such are the much-altered main range at Summerlee (the former Hydrocon Crane works), the maintenance workshops at the Dalmellington Ironworks, and the relocated Linthouse engine works at the Scottish Maritime Museum. At Dalmellington the intention is to display tools appropriate to the original use of the building as a locomotive and general repair shop. The related (but mainly woodworking) wagon repair shop at Dalmellington has also been restored.

The most characteristic piece of ironfounders' plant is the cupola furnace used for remelting iron, but though many old cupolas survived into the 1970s, none has been preserved. Falkirk

Museum has, however, a good collection of moulding boxes, metal ladles and smaller items used in the industry. Summerlee also has some ironfounding equipment, and its displays include a brassfounder's shop. The other related trade of steelfounding is represented at Summerlee by the sole surviving Tropenas converter, used for making steel in small quantities from pig-iron.

Shipbuilding is perhaps Scotland's most celebrated industry. It developed on the Clyde and on the east coast during the 18th and 19th centuries, though on a small scale. The real impetus came after steamship construction after 1812. At first, engines and boilers were made by specialists and installed in wooden hulls built in traditional yards, but from the 1830s iron hulls came into favour, and there was an increasing tendency for engine and boilermaking to be integrated with hull construction. The Clyde took a lead in building first-class steamships which it never lost: by the time Clyde shipbuilding declined, motorships were the norm. It is of the nature of ships that they are large, often very large, and shipyards correspondingly sizeable. It is not surprising, therefore, that no attempt has been made to preserve a shipbuilding yard. The industry is thus generally represented by builders' models, of which Glasgow has the finest collection, though many other museums contain examples. The McLean museum in Greenock has displays on shipbuilding, as do Dundee Museum, Clydebank Museum and the Aberdeen Maritime Museum. The Scottish Maritime Museum at Irvine has acquired a good collection of shipbuilding machine tools which it plans to display in the re-erected Linthouse engine works. The Maritime Museum also runs the Denny Ship Model Experiment Tank at Dumbarton, where models were used in the design of full-sized ships. The preservation of individual ships is dealt with in the transport section of this introduction. As with engineering, shipbuilding in Scotland has declined markedly since the 1960s, but the surviving firms in Glasgow and Port Glasgow are proving successful.

It is worth remembering that collections made, or sites preserved for other reasons may contain items made by specialised industries. In a distillery, for example, there may be examples of the art of the coppersmith (stills and worms or condensers), brass worker (spirit safe), vat builder (tuns and spirit receivers), cooper (casks), and ironfounder (chargers and low wines receiver, mash tun). In a watermill there will be millwright work in iron and wood, with the waterwheel often locally made. In a textile mill the preparation machinery, spinning machines and looms are all engineering products, though seldom of Scottish make. It is always worth looking at objects preserved ostensibly for one reason to see what other meanings they have.

SCOTLAND'S TRANSPORT HISTORY IN SITES AND MUSEUMS

Visitors to Scotland may well be impressed by its spectacular scenery of mountains and moorland, rivers and lochs, forests and islands, but for the civil engineers who developed various modes of transport over the centuries, Scotland represented a hostile environment. The choice of routes was limited by the terrain, so roads and railways often followed the course of a convenient river. On the other hand, some major river estuaries presented an obstacle which had to be overcome by a ferry – until long bridges could be built.

Another feature of Scotland, often underestimated by visitors, is its size. When a traveller from London to John o'Groats via Gretna Green enters Scotland, the journey has not yet reached the half-way mark. The sparsity of towns and villages is notable in all but the central Lowlands – a fact which reduced the demand, and finance, for transport systems over the years. For island communities the transport problems were even greater.

ROAD TRANSPORT

In England, the Romans built an extensive network of roads, but in Scotland their influence was far less significant. Three north–south roads were built to service the Antonine Wall which ran from the Forth to the Clyde, and one of these ventured further north to service isolated outposts. Scotland's early travellers developed a system of drove roads which sufficed until the introduction of coaches in the 16th century.

In 1610 a passenger coach service was inaugurated between Edinburgh and Leith but journeys were slow and uncomfortable. In 1678 a coach journey from Edinburgh to Glasgow took six days, but the establishment of turnpike (toll) roads from the early 1700s improved standards and cut travelling time. Following the Jacobite uprising of 1715, General George Wade was given the task of building an improved network of roads in the Highlands to allow troops to move quickly and suppress any further uprisings. Towards the end of the century, improved methods of constructing the surface of roads were introduced by three famous engineers: two of these were Scots, John Loudon Macadam and Thomas Telford, and the other was a colourful character from Yorkshire called 'Blind' Jack Metcalfe of Knaresborough, who built many roads in the north of England despite his blindness. Macadam produced a cheap, but good, surface – not using tar, which came much later; Telford and another great Scottish engineer, John Rennie, built numerous bridges still in use today.

In 1838, a famous Scottish lawyer Lord Brougham ordered a new high-quality town carriage, which proved to be very popular and was named after him. In 1846 a very unusual Brougham was designed with pneumatic tyres. The usual date given for this invention is 1888, when another Scottish inventor John Boyd Dunlop produced a successful pneumatic tyre for a bicycle. The Brougham's tyres were produced by a Stonehaven engineer Robert William Thomson, but they were not a commercial success. Thomson had more success with his steam-powered road vehicles in the second half of the 19th century. The pedal-operated bicycle was invented by a Scottish blacksmith called Kirkpatrick Macmillan in about 1840. Macmillan, from Courthill in Dumfriesshire, developed his machine from a hobby-horse by fitting pedals connected by links and cranks to the rear wheel.

At the end of the 19th century road transport changed dramatically; horse trams were replaced by cable trams and then electric trams. The first motor cars appeared, and motor buses replaced horse and steam buses. During the first half of the 20th century there was a steady improvement in vehicles and roads but around the middle of the century there were some major changes: trams disappeared, motorways were constructed, and some spectacular bridges were built, including those across the Firths of Forth, Tay and Clyde.

SEA TRAVEL

Scotland's mountainous hinterland and the multitude of islands off the north and west coasts have resulted in a long history of sea travel as the most common form of transport for the many people living on or near the coast. Obviously, those living on the islands relied upon ferries to get across to the mainland or to other islands, but a resident of Edinburgh wishing to travel to London in around 1800 often went by sea, since the stage coach journey was slow and uncomfortable, while there was a good service from Leith to London in fast sailing smacks. Heavy goods almost always had to travel by sea. By the 1830s, steam packets were becoming popular for this profitable coastal trade.

The Shetland Museum's Ness yoal Maggie *(right) sailing off Virkie, Dunrossness. (see p.116)*

Scottish inventors also played a major role in the transition from sail to steam. Although James Watt revolutionized the steam engine, his bulky low-pressure engines were too cumbersome even for ships. William Symington, who had worked on stationary Boulton and Watt engines in Scotland during the 18th century and later developed his own designs for high-pressure engines, was asked to provide one of these engines for a paddle-driven boat owned by a wealthy banker, Patrick Miller. The boat was tested on Dalswinton Loch in 1788 and was a limited success. A second boat followed, and was succeeded by the further improved *Charlotte Dundas*, which towed two large barges on the Forth and Clyde Canal during 1803. Some years later, in 1812, Henry Bell of Helensburgh built his paddle steamer *Comet*, which was used to operate the first commercial steamboat service in Britain. The transition from paddle to screw propeller took place later in the 19th century – one of the pioneers being Robert Wilson of Dunbar with his experiments of 1826.

Probably the most famous Scottish services of the era of steam were those operated by the paddle steamers on the River Clyde, and the 'Puffers' serving the Highlands and Islands. Less glamorous, but nevertheless vital, were the many ferry boats which made their crossing points famous – Erskine, Renfrew, Queensferry, Ballachulish – until they were replaced by bridges. Despite the competition of air travel, ferries to many of the islands still operate today.

CANALS

Scotland never had a network of canals similar to that built in England during the later years of the 18th century. Due to the terrain, Scotland's canals tended to be built in an east–west direction, making use of river valleys. The obvious target for the canal builders was a link between the rivers Forth and Clyde. Two routes were surveyed, one by John Smeaton and the other by James Watt; Smeaton's was chosen and the canal opened in 1790 from Bowling on the Clyde to Grangemouth on the Forth. There was a branch into Glasgow, and in 1822 the Union Canal was opened from the eastern end of the Forth and Clyde Canal into the heart of Edinburgh. 'Swift boats' carried passengers between Glasgow and Edinburgh, but their success was short-lived, declining when the towns were linked by rail in 1842.

The other major canal in Scotland, the Caledonian Canal, linked the east and west coasts by taking ships through the Great Glen from Inverness to Fort William, providing an attractive alternative to a journey through the stormy waters around the north of Scotland. Engineered by Thomas Telford, and opened after many delays in 1822, the canal linked three lochs, including Loch Ness.

Several short industrial canals were built, but most of these were also eventually superseded by the railways; for example, the Monkland Canal, built by James Watt to carry coal into Glasgow. The Crinan Canal, designed by John Rennie and opened in 1801, linked the Sound of Jura on the west coast with Loch Fyne. This allowed boats from the north to take a short-cut to Glasgow by avoiding the long haul round the Mull of Kintyre. Fishing boats and puffers were frequent users of the Crinan Canal which is still open today.

Brechin Railway Station, Angus. (see p.32)

RAILWAYS

The first railway in Scotland was the wagonway built in 1722 to carry coal from Tranent in East Lothian to the coast at Cockenzie. Gravity and horses provided the power. This railway receives another mention in some history books, for the Battle of Prestonpans was fought across its track during the Jacobite uprising of 1745. Many wagonways using horses were built – usually to transport coal, but the Kilmarnock and Troon Railway operated a limited passenger service in about 1817. A steam locomotive was reputedly tested with little success.

In 1831 the Monkland and Kirkintilloch Railway introduced two steam locomotives on their track; these were the first of many locomotives to be built in Scotland. During the next two decades railways were built at an amazing rate. Glasgow and Edinburgh were linked in 1842 and by 1848 passengers could travel from London to Glasgow and Edinburgh. The Scottish section of this west coast route was operated by the Caledonian Railway, founded in 1845. The east coast route from Edinburgh to Berwick-upon-Tweed was opened by the North British Railway, and by 1850 through services to London were available. Great rivalry developed between the east and west coast routes, culminating in the famous 'races' of 1888. At 10 o'clock each day trains left Kings Cross and Euston and raced to Edinburgh. The record time was set on the east coast route at 7 hours 27 minutes but eventually a truce was called.

As the North British Railway extended to the north it was faced by the firths of Forth and Tay, and ferries continued to be used until the great bridges were built. The Tay Bridge was opened in 1878 but collapsed soon afterwards during a great storm. Re-designed, it reopened in 1887. The magnificent Forth Bridge opened in 1890.

Regional networks grew during the latter half of the 19th century: the central belt was covered by the Caledonian Railway in the west and the North British Railway in the east, with the Glasgow and South Western Railway, the Highland Railway, and the Great North of Scotland Railway covering the regions mentioned in their titles.

Since the streets of Glasgow had become very congested, even in the 1880s, an underground railway was proposed. Work started in 1891 and by 1896 the Glasgow District Subway was opened. The original trains were hauled by endless cables powered by stationary steam engines, but in 1933 the decision was taken to electrify the system. After a roof-fall in 1977 it was decided to rebuild the system completely and the new 'Clockwork Orange' trains began to carry passengers in 1980.

The 20th century has seen the 1923 'grouping' of the many operating railways into four companies: LNER, LMS, SR and GWR. In 1948 these companies were nationalized as British Railways and then in 1963 came Dr Beeching's 'Re-Shaping' report which resulted in the closure of many branch lines. On the technical side, diesel locomotives replaced steam during the 1950s and during the 1970s electrification spread. By 1974 the west coast route from London to Glasgow had been electrified and later the east coast route followed suit.

AIR TRAVEL

Britain's first balloon flight and first successful glider flight were both made in Scotland: the former by James Tytler from Edinburgh in 1784, and the latter by Percy Pilcher during 1895 when he flew his gliders on the slopes above the north bank of the River Clyde. Following the first successful aeroplane, built by the Wright brothers in the United States during 1903, a number of Scottish pioneers built aeroplanes and flew as a sport. During World War I many airships were based along the east coast to protect the fleet by spotting enemy warships. William Beardmore and Company built several large rigid airships at Inchinnan, near Glasgow, including the R34 which made the first east to west crossing of the Atlantic by air: it departed from East Fortune in East Lothian in July 1919 and flew non-stop to New York making the return flight to England a few days later.

The first Scottish scheduled air services commenced in 1933, which coincided with similar operations south of the border. There were two great rivals operating in the Highlands and Islands during the early years. Captain Fresson's Highland Airways started a service from Inverness to Wick and Kirkwall in May 1933 while Eric Leslie Gandar Dower's Allied Airways flew services from Aberdeen to Glasgow, Edinburgh, and the northern islands from 1934. In addition to passenger services, airmail was carried and from 1934 Captain Fresson started air ambulance flights in the northern islands. Flights from Glasgow to Campbeltown and Islay also started in 1933 and services to the western islands extended and expanded to include airmail and air ambulance flights.

Services were curtailed during World War II and after the war the small independent airlines were all taken over by British European Airways which, in turn, became part of British Airways.

Museum of Transport, Glasgow. (see p.87)

MUSEUMS AND SITES

ABERDEEN MARITIME MUSEUM

**Provost Ross's House,
Shiprow, Aberdeen
Tel: (01224) 337700**

Open: *Monday to Friday, 10am to 5pm*
Sunday, 11am to 5pm.

Admission: *Free*

Refreshments: *Tea Room*

Parking: *None*

Disabled access: *Access to all floors, toilet*

The Maritime Museum is just one of a number of museums and galleries run by the local authority in Aberdeen. Within this group are several collections of transport-related material, not necessarily on display, but available for study purposes and used for special exhibitions. Paintings, photographs and archives cover road, rail, air and, of course, sea travel. The aviation archive material relating to the Scottish airline pioneer Eric Leslie Gander Dower and Dyce Airport are of particular interest. Larger objects include a stage coach, a Lister truck and several cycles. Queries on this material should be directed to the Art Gallery, Schoolhill, Aberdeen AB9 1FQ. Telephone (01224) 646333.

The Maritime Museum is housed in the city's oldest surviving building, Provost Ross's house, which overlooks the harbour. The original house was built in 1593 and later joined to the adjacent house. Provost Ross, who occupied the premises during the 18th century, was a merchant with business interests in the harbour and shipping. The building was derelict in 1954, but The National Trust for Scotland restored it and now lease it to the museum. From one of the windows, visitors can view the harbour and a regularly updated notice gives information on the ships which can be seen. Many of these are involved in North Sea oil and gas industries for which Aberdeen is an important base.

SHIPPING

The collection of complete ship models on display numbers about 120, plus some 55 half-models used by the shipbuilder to show the shape of the hull. The small rooms of the historic building limit the size of objects which can be displayed but good use is made of the available space. Aberdeen Art Gallery has a fine collection of paintings including many with a maritime theme, so it is not surprising to find these featured in the Maritime Museum. Perhaps the most impressive is *The Herring Fleet Leaving the Dee* by David Farquharson, 1888. Good use is also made of early photographs which often capture the atmosphere far better than words ever can.

Because of the difficult terrain in the north of Scotland, with its Highlands and Islands, sea travel was widely used throughout the 19th century and even into the 20th century. The 'North Boats' linked Aberdeen with coastal ports and the islands of Shetland and Orkney, while the 'London Boats' carried passengers and cargo to the south. The story of these services is well told with models, photographs and paintings.

INDUSTRY

Aberdeen harbour is man-made, built on the shallow estuary of the River Dee. An interesting display tells the story of the development of the harbour from post-medieval times to the present day. There have been many changes in the industries served by the harbour: lime, timber, coal, fishing, whaling and, more recently, oil and gas.

The shipbuilding industry in Aberdeen was founded in the mid 18th century and for 200 years was a major contributor to Aberdeen's prosperity. The shipbuilding display highlights the great days of the Aberdeen-built clipper ships, such as the record-breaking *Thermopylae*, with illustrations and models. Two large collections of ship drawings, one from Hall Russell & Co. and the other from John Lewis & Sons, are in the care of the museum. These are catalogued and available for research purposes by prior appointment.

An audio-visual presentation tells the story of the North Sea oil and gas industries and there is a very large and detailed model of the Murchison Oilfield production platform. The actual platform built in 1980 is still in use – but not easy to visit.

ABERFELDY WATER MILL

Aberfeldy,
Perthshire & Kinross
Tel: (01887) 820803

Open: *Easter to October*

Admission: *Charges*

Refreshments: *Tea Room*

Parking: *None at mill, but available on streets nearby*

Disabled access: *Limited*

A meal mill built in a style characteristic of the Breadalbane estate, Aberfeldy Mill dates from 1826 and though the kiln has been remodelled, most recently in the early post-war period, in other respects it is little altered externally. The millstones were removed some years ago, but stone grinding equipment was re-inserted in the 1980s, driven by the surviving water wheel. The mill is now operated as a visitor attraction, with a video, display panels, restaurant and guided tours.

Aberfeldy Mill, Perthshire, before restoration and opening to the public. (Above)

Glass cone, Alloa, Clackmannanshire. As built, the glass furnace sat behind the stone arches in the base, the brick cone acting as a chimney. (Right)

ALLOA GLASS CONE

Alloa,
Clackmannanshire

View from footpath

The survivor of a pair of cones on this site, the Alloa Glass Cone is within the United Glass bottle factory in Alloa. This is a lineal descendant of the Alloa Glass Company, founded in the middle of the 18th century. The surviving cone dates from about 1825 and is the only one left in Scotland.

ALMOND VALLEY HERITAGE CENTRE AND LIVINGSTON MILL

Livingston, West Lothian
Tel: (01506) 414957

Open: *Daily*

Admission: *Charges*

Refreshments: *Tea room*

Parking: *Car and coach park*

Disabled access: *Good in Heritage Centre, not easy in Mill*

The Almond Valley Heritage Centre has been established by Livingston New Town Development Corporation. Its primary objective is the presentation of the history of the extraction of oil from shale, an industry which flourished in West Lothian from the 1850s to the 1950s. The Scottish pioneer of shale oil production, James 'Paraffin' Young, developed many of the techniques for oil refining which are still used. The displays include a re-creation of a mine interior, as well as artifacts, models and images depicting the industry and the society it created. The setting is a purpose-built museum building, adjacent to Livingston Mill (see below), and outdoor attractions include farm implements and a narrow-gauge railway.

Livingston Mill was the water-powered corn mill for the village and parish of Livingston until into this century. After a period of disuse, it was rescued by a group of enthusiasts in the late 1960s. They rebuilt the waterwheel and overhauled the machinery, which now works. The interior of the mill has been adapted to show visitors how it worked.

Horse-drawn paraffin tanker in the Almond Valley Heritage Centre, Livingston, West Lothian. The shale-oil industry interpreted here, based its fortunes on lamp oil production.

Farm machinery at Livingston Mill Farm, Almond Valley Heritage Centre, with a horse-drawn hay rake in the foreground.

The signal tower built by the Northern Lighthouse Board for communicating with the Bell Rock Lighthouse, with houses for the keepers' families.
It now houses the Arbroath Museum. (Below)

ARBROATH MUSEUM

Signal Tower, Ladyloan, Arbroath, Angus
Tel: (01241) 875598

Open: *All year, Monday to Saturday; July and August, Sunday p.m.*

Admission: *Free*

Refreshments: *None*

Parking: *Car park*

Disabled access: *Limited, downstairs only*

The museum building was the signal tower for the Bell Rock Lighthouse situated some 11 miles (18 km) off Arbroath. For lighthouses in sight of the shore, a tower was often built from which visual signals could be sent in the days before radio communication. This complex was also home for the wives and families. The Bell or Inchcape Rock was a treacherous rock, particularly for shipping using the River Tay or sailing up the east coast. In 1811 a lighthouse was erected on the rocks to the design of Robert Stevenson (grandfather of the writer Robert Louis Stevenson). The light is now automatic, but the work of the lighthouse keeper is

commemorated in the museum with two displays including the last manually operated light and the figure of a lighthouse keeper who, at the touch of a button, tells the visitor about the lighthouse. Another display features a 3-D cross-sectional model of the lighthouse.

Displays of local industries include fishing, from which the famous Arbroath 'smokie' (smoked haddock) is produced, and marine-related trades: shipbuilding, engineering and sail-making. One of the items in the collection is an inverted vertical steam engine made by Shanks of Arbroath for the Dunoon Gasworks, where it worked until the early 1970s.

The museum's major industrial focus is on the flax industry which produced canvas, osnaburg cloth and sail cloth. The quality of the latter is borne out by the inventor of the successful pneumatic tyre, John Boyd Dunlop, whose description of his method of construction said '. . . and the cloth portion of the cover, which was made of the finest quality of yacht sail cloth, was manufactured in Arbroath'.

ARBUTHNOT MUSEUM, PETERHEAD

St Peter Street, Peterhead, Aberdeenshire
Tel: (01779) 477778

Open: *All year, closed Sundays*

Admission: *Free*

Refreshments: *None*

Parking: *Public car park nearby*

Disabled access: *Difficult – stairs*

The Arbuthnot Museum is named after Adam Arbuthnot, a Peterhead merchant who retired in 1820 and devoted 30 years to building up his collections of coins, natural history and curiosities. Today, it also serves as the headquarters of the North East of Scotland Museums Service which supports museums in Banff, Banchory, Huntly, Inverurie, Maud and Stonehaven. The Carnegie Museum at Inverurie has a small display on the local

canal. The Great North of Scotland Railway, which had large workshops at Inverurie, is featured in a railway exhibition in the former station building at Maud, 13 miles (22 km) west of Peterhead. (**Huntly** has a short entry in the Appendix and the **Tolbooth Museum** at Stonehaven has a separate entry.)

Peterhead grew up around the whaling and fishing industries and these are featured, with ship models, artifacts and photographs. Other industries covered by the displays include: weaving, shipbuilding, cooperage and quarrying. The latter is an unusual topic for a museum display, but the well-known granite quarries at nearby Boddam were very important to both Peterhead and Aberdeen (the 'Granite City').

AUCHINDRAIN OLD HIGHLAND TOWNSHIP

Near Furnace, Argyll
Tel: (014995) 235

Open: *April to September, daily, except Saturdays in April, May and September*

Admission: *Charges*

Refreshments: *Tea room*

Parking: *Car and coach park*

Disabled access: *Fair*

The joint-tenancy farm of Auchindrain, between Inveraray and Furnace on Loch Fyne, is a remarkable survival in terms of land tenure and the buildings associated with it. Though of significance primarily for agricultural and social history there are a number of items of industrial interest, including farm machinery – ploughs, harrows, drills – and, unusually, a massive salt-glazed stoneware pickling tub from one of the Ayrshire heavy ceramic works. The implements were all designed for small farms, making an interesting contrast with the larger equipment found in other agricultural museums. There is also a smiddy, but this is inappropriately set in a former barn.

AULD KIRK MUSEUM

(see entry for **Barony Chambers Museum**)

Thatched cottage and byre, Auchindrain Old Highland Township, Argyll. (Upper)

Cart wheel on iron tyring ring at Auchindrain. (Lower)

BARONY CHAMBERS MUSEUM AND AULD KIRK MUSEUM

Kirkintilloch, East Dunbartonshire
Tel: (0141) 775 1185

Open: *Tuesday, Thursday, Friday and Saturday afternoons and Saturday mornings*

Admission: *Free*

Refreshments: *None*

Parking: *No formal*

Disabled access: *Stairs*

East Dunbartonshire Council has two museums in Kirkintilloch, both in important historic buildings. The first of these was the Auld Kirk Museum, in a 17th-century church, and the Barony Chambers Museum followed in the Georgian Town House. It is the latter that is concerned with Kirkintilloch's industries, among other aspects of life in the burgh. For a place of its size, Kirkintilloch has had a very varied industrial history. The handloom weaving and coal mining so characteristic of the west of Scotland were there, but so was a notable architectural ironfounding industry, and canal related trades, especially ship building and repair. Chemical manufacture and distilling also had their place. Key factors in this industrial diversity were the Forth and Clyde Canal, which reached here from the east in 1776, and the Monkland and Kirkintilloch Railway (1826), Scotland's first 'modern' railway. Displays illustrate weaving, mining, ironfounding, the canal and the railway. By the canal at the Townhead is an air hammer from the nearby Star Foundry, preserved in the open air.

BARONY COLLIERY

Near Auchinleck, East Ayrshire

View from road only

This was the first really large and deep pit in Ayrshire, and was chosen by the National Coal Board for one of the first new sinkings after nationalisation of the coal industry in 1947. The original winding engine houses and power station of the old shafts were still in existence when the pit closed in 1990, but it was only possible to save the headframe of the early 1950s sinking from the site clearance that followed closure. This giant steel A frame, of German design, was built in Glasgow, and is a striking memorial to large-scale mining in an important coalfield. It contrasts markedly in scale and style with the headgear at **Highhouse** colliery in Auchinleck.

The giant A-frame headgear at Barony Colliery, Auchinleck, shown here before demolition of the surrounding buildings.

BARRY MILL

Barry, Angus
Tel: (01241) 856761

Open: *May to mid October, daily*

Admission: *Charges*

Refreshments: *None*

Parking: *Yes*

Disabled access: *Limited*

Barry Mill, the last Angus watermill to work commercially, was acquired by The National Trust for Scotland in the late 1980s, and was opened to the public in 1992. It was one of a series of mills in Barry, and is one of a group of Angus mills with circular kilns. Its two pairs of stones and overshot wheel are thoroughly typical of a later 19th-century developed oatmeal mill.

Barry Mill, Angus in the 1970's.

BENHOLM MILL

Benholm, Aberdeenshire
Tel: None

Open: *Spring 1995*

Admission: *Charges*

Refreshments: *Will have tea room*

Parking: *For cars and coaches*

Disabled access: *Not known*

This was the last working water mill in Kincardineshire, and one of the smallest mills to work into the 1970s. During the early 1990s it was restored by volunteers from the Scottish Conservation Projects Trust with a view to public access from the spring of 1995. The mill, dating largely from the early 19th century, has two pairs of stones driven by a small wood and iron overshot wheel.

Benholm Mill, Kincardineshire, after restoration but before opening to the public.

BIGGAR GASWORKS

Biggar, South Lanarkshire
Tel: (0131) 668 8600

Open: *May to September, daily*

Admission: *Free*

Refreshments: *None*

Parking: Small car park, no coaches

Disabled access: *Good*

When the Biggar Gas Works closed in 1973 it was one of the last to make gas from coal in Scotland, and largely on the initiative of the Biggar Museum Trust, the works were taken into the care of the Secretary of State for Scotland. The fabric of the works has been maintained by Historic Scotland and its predecessors, while the machinery and plant in the works were looked after by the then Royal Scottish Museum. The Museum also introduced a number of objects from other gas works, including two steam engines, a gas engine, and a small steam locomotive from Granton Gas Works in Edinburgh as well as displays on the domestic use of gas, in the former showroom.

The most important aspect of the works is, however, its survival as a complete coal-fuelled gas works of a type once found in towns and villages throughout the United Kingdom. Only three now survive, the others being at Fakenham in Norfolk and Carrickfergus in Northern Ireland.

Biggar Gas Works was opened in 1836. The old retort house still stands, but the rest of the works has been modified over the years. As it is today, it has almost all the features of a country gas works of the middle part of this century. From the coal store, coal was charged by hand into horizontal retorts, where heat decomposed the coal into gas, coke, and a mixture of liquids, including tar and ammonia liquor. These liquids, which were drawn out of the retorts in vapour form, were removed in two stages by condensers and a scrubber and washer, the last impurity, hydrogen sulphide, being taken out in box-shaped purifiers. The pure gas was then stored in two cylindrical steel gas holders and fed into main pipes to suppliers through a large gas meter. The

coke was sold locally as a cheap fuel and the tar taken away for refining into saleable products.

The works has deliberately been kept very much as it was when it closed, the only major change being the loss of the chimney. It provides an opportunity to see a part of rural life now vanished.

Charging a retort in a coal-carbonising gas works. This photograph was taken at Maybole gasworks, but the equipment and technique at Biggar were identical. (Upper)

The retort house at Biggar Gasworks. (Lower)

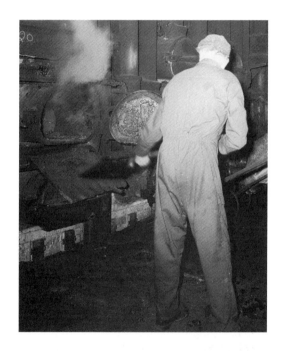

BIGGAR MUSEUM TRUST

Moat Park Heritage Centre, Biggar, South Lanarkshire
Tel: (01899) 221050

Open: *Easter to October (offices all year round)*

Admission: *Charges*

Refreshments: *Light refreshments, good food nearby*

Parking: *At Moat Park and public car parks nearby*

Disabled access: *Access and facilities good*

An Albion motor car of 1902 (not 1900) with a dogcart layout of seats.

GLADSTONE COURT MUSEUM

The Biggar Museum Trust was a pioneer in Scotland of a modern approach to voluntary provision of museum services. Brian Lambie, his trustees and volunteers have created a remarkable and unusual group of museums in Biggar and Broughton, including the Gladstone Court Museum, a notable street museum, which includes an ironmonger's store, a bank, photographer, chemist, dressmaker, watchmaker, milliner, printer and bootmaker, together with a village library, schoolroom and even the switchboard from the old manual telephone exchange in the village.

When the local gasworks closed down in 1973 the Biggar Museum Trust led the way to ensure its preservation (*see* **Biggar Gasworks**).

TRANSPORT

The Museum Trust's interest in transport history centres on the fact that one of the two founders of the great Albion Motor Car Company was born in Biggar in 1871. Thomas Blackwood Murray's family owned the farm of Heavyside at Biggar and his father was one of Scotland's first car owners. Thomas Blackwood Murray and his brother-in-law Norman Fulton founded the Albion Company in Glasgow during 1899, with a bond on the farm of some £1,300. The company grew into a major manufacturer of commercial vehicles and became part of the Leyland Group of Companies in 1951. The name was dropped in 1972 but, following a management buy-out of the axle plant at Scotstoun, the name and famous logo are once more to be seen as Albion Automotive.

The chassis and engine of the first Albion built in 1900 is preserved in the **Museum of Transport,** Glasgow while the second, a dogcart car which belonged to Mr Murray of Heavyside, is in the collection of the **Royal Museum of Scotland,** Edinburgh. In 1990 the Biggar Museum Trust purchased another dogcart dating from 1902 which had been part of a collection in Hawaii, and is now on display in Biggar. The Trust also owns a 1923 Albion Hotel Bus used in the original 'Dr Finlay' series on television, a unique travelling home built in 1938 on a 1936 AZ Albion chassis, and several other Albion commercial vehicles including tipper lorries of 1931 and 1938 and an army truck of 1943.

Of particular interest to automobile historians is the Albion Archive housed near Gladstone Court, one of the Trust's three museums in Biggar. This vast archive contains over 164,000 job sheets, the company records and minute books, photographs, service manuals and spares lists. Access to the archive is by appointment only.

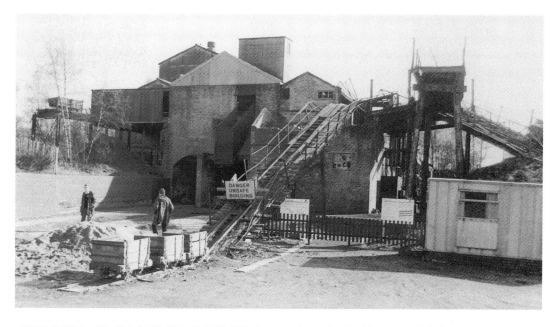

BIRKHILL CLAY MINE, BO'NESS DEVELOPMENT TRUST

Near Bo'ness, Falkirk
Tel: (01506) 825855

Open: *April to mid July and September to October weekends only. Mid July to August daily*

Admission: *Charges*

Refreshments: *None*

Parking: *At Bo'ness train connection, and at mine*

Disabled access: *Not suitable for disabled visitors*

The Birkhill Clay Mine was operated by P. & M. Hurll, manufacturers of refractory (heat-resisting) bricks. High quality fireclay occurs throughout central Scotland, and Birkhill was one of a fair number of such mines. It was the last to operate, and after it closed in the early 1900s it was acquired by the Bo'ness Heritage Trust and adapted to allow visitors to go underground. The clay was worked by 'stoop and room', with pillars left to support the roof, and it provides a dramatic experience. When in use, the clay was hauled out of the mine up a long narrow-gauge railway incline to a crushing and loading plant. These features still survive, but are not currently accessible to the

The surface buildings at Birkhill clay mine, near Bo'ness, West Lothian, where the clay from the mine was crushed before shipment to the brickworks.

public. The mine is best reached by train from Bo'ness to Birkhill Station, which is immediately adjacent to the crushing and loading plant, which was originally rail-served. The mine is now operated by the Bo'ness Development Trust.

BLAIR ATHOLL MILL

Blair Atholl Mill, Perthshire & Kinross
Tel: (01796) 481321

Open: *April (or Easter) to October, daily*

Admission: *Charges*

Refreshments: *Tea room*

Parking: *Good car park*

Disabled access: *Limited*

Built as an estate corn mill in 1831, using the rubble masonry characteristic of the Duke of Atholl's model village, this mill was disused for many years before being brought back into use by John Ridley in partnership with the Atholl Estate. The machinery has been thoroughly refurbished so that the oatmeal produced can be sold for human consumption, and the interior of the buildings has been adapted for visitor circulation and facilities. This was the first water mill in Scotland developed as a commercial tourist attraction.

The low-breast water wheel at Blair Atholl mill which drives the millstones which grind oatmeal at the mill.

BÖD (BOOTH) OF GREMISTA, LERWICK

Lerwick, Shetland
Correspondence to: Shetland Museum, Lower Hillhead,
Lerwick, Shetland
Tel: (01595) 695057 or 694386
Fax: (01595) 696729

Open: *June to September, Wednesday to Sunday*

Admission: *Charges*

Refreshments: *None*

Parking: *Car park*

Disabled access: *Ground floor only, toilet*

This small but interesting museum is housed in an 18th century house, known as The Böd (Norse for 'Booth') of Gremista on the west shore of Bressay Sound near the P. & O. Terminal. The ferry terminal is used by the regular P. & O. ferries from Aberdeen – and other vessels. The P. & O. company is of special significance in these parts because one

of its founders, Arthur Anderson, was born in the Böd of Gremista in 1792. After serving in the Royal Navy during the Napoleonic Wars, Anderson and his partner Brodie M. Willcox supplied the Royalists during the Portuguese and Spanish civil wars of 1828 and 1832.

In 1833, Anderson and Willcox used their experience of the Iberian peninsula to found the Peninsular Steam Navigation Company. They were innovative in their reliance on steam ships and a model of their first paddle steamer, the *William Fawcett*, is displayed in the P. & O. Room of the Museum. In 1840 the original company won a contract to carry mail to Alexandria in Egypt and later to India which resulted in an expansion of their operations and the founding of the Peninsular and Oriental Steam Navigation Company. On display is a print of the paddle steamer *Hindostan*'s departure for India in 1842. There is also a model of the mid-19th-century P. & O. steamer the *Himalaya*. Although most of the displays relate to Anderson, the man, they do give an insight into the founding of a shipping company which played a major role in transport history.

The rest of the house is fitted out in period style. On the ground floor, originally the salt cellar, there are displays of items associated with line fishing and the subsequent processing of the fish.

BONAWE IRONWORKS

Taynuilt, Argyll & Bute
Tel: (01866) 822432

Open: *April to September*

Admission: *Charges*

Refreshments: *None*

Parking: *Car parking, no coaches*

Disabled access: *Good, though not on lade walk*

Bonawe Ironworks is a remarkable survival from the 18th century. Founded in 1753 by Richard Ford & Co., otherwise the Newland Furnace Company, with works near Ulverston in Furness, Bonawe was one of a small group of charcoal-

The blast furnace at Bonawe Ironworks.

fuelled iron smelting works built in the Highlands of Scotland from the 1720s to the 1750s. The attraction for all was large tracts of natural broad-leafed woodland which could be cut for charcoal, and good reliable water power. These natural resources could be used to make what was then a high-value product which could stand the considerable transport costs of moving iron ore from England and returning the iron to that country. Those works – Bonawe and the Argyll Furnace at Furnace, Lochfyneside – which were most successful, could rely on sea transport not only to move ore and iron, but also to mobilise supplies of charcoal.

Though the value of iron fell as coke smelting was introduced into Scotland, first at Carron in 1760, then in a group of ironworks founded in the last quarter of the 18th century, Bonawe continued to prosper. The dramatic reduction in prices that accompanied the introduction of the hot-blast process in the 1830s and 40s left Bonawe unscathed. It was by that time a minute unit relative to the great Lanarkshire or Ayrshire works, such as Gartsherrie and Summerlee, but it had a niche in the market for high-quality iron. For a number of years before it closed in the mid 1870s (the exact year is not known), its output was used primarily to make iron castings for treatment with powdered iron ore to turn them into 'malleable iron castings', resistant to sudden shock. The end of the works came at a time of recession after the end of the Franco-Prussian War, which coincided with the running out of some of the woodland leases. The company retreated to their original base at Newland, where they continued to make iron under Bonawe's brand name 'Lorn' until the turn of the century.

The buildings at Bonawe were well constructed of massive granite blocks, and had durable roofs covered with Lakeland slates. They found new uses for agricultural storage, and though the buildings round the base of the furnace were torn down to make flood-protection works in the early years of this century, the others survived almost intact into the 1960s. By that time Bonawe was a name known to schoolchildren throughout Scotland, and interest in the remains was developing. The growing interest in industrial archaeology of the 1960s was the trigger to active work to preserve what remained at Bonawe.

Even in decay, this was undeniably impressive. Set among giant, over-mature ash trees was the furnace, its lining ripped out in the 1870s, its roof disintegrating, its cast-iron lintels flaking, but still marked BUNAW F 1753. Behind were the two massive charcoal sheds, set into the hillside, and an ore shed with verandah. These have all been restored, and laid out for visiting, with displays in the ore shed and furnace charging house. The area round the furnace has been excavated and the working spaces clearly labelled. Visitors may walk up the lade to the River Awe. The site is in the care of Historic Scotland.

BO'NESS AND KINNEIL RAILWAY

Bo'ness Station, Union Street, Bo'ness, Falkirk

Tel: (01506) 822298

Fax: (01506) 828766

Open: *Easter to mid October and December, Saturday and Sunday, July and August daily*

Special events: *confirm by phone*

Admission: *Fare for train journey*

Refreshments: *Café*

Parking: *Large car park*

Disabled access: *Ramp to station, toilet. (Assistance available for access to trains)*

The Bo'ness (Borrowstounness) and Kinneil Railway is run by the Scottish Railway Preservation Society which is a volunteer organisation founded in 1961. After many years operating from inadequate premises in Falkirk, they took the decision to move to a 'green field' site at Bo'ness. The main site is on the foreshore of the Firth of Forth and adjacent to the disused harbour and 19th-century dock – Bo'ness was once Scotland's second largest port.

The move from Falkirk to Bo'ness commenced in 1979 and involved major construction work, putting up buildings and laying track. One of the first buildings to be moved onto the site was the station from Wormit in Fife, originally built in 1887 when the rebuilt Tay Bridge was opened. An even earlier building was the ornate cast-iron train shed which came from Haymarket Station in Edinburgh where it was built in 1842 for the opening of the Edinburgh and Glasgow Railway. Many of the other structures needed for a working railway were moved from their original sites to Bo'ness including: a signal box, footbridge, crane and water column. The locomotive shed is a modern building but built in the style of the old North British Railway and using window frames recovered from an old railway building in Glasgow.

Laying the railway track may have been less conspicuous than the erection of buildings but it was absolutely essential and involved much hard work by the volunteer workers. By 1986 they were able to operate trains to Kinneil Halt, about a mile away. This is the site of the former Kinneil Colliery and nearby is Kinneil House where James Watt built his first full-scale steam engine in 1769. Two years later the line was extended a further two miles to the **Birkhill Fireclay Mine**, which is open to visitors. In addition to the industrial history of the area and the impressive view of the Grangemouth oil refinery, there are some fine scenic views across the Firth of Forth to the mountains of the Highlands – even to Ben Lomond on a clear day.

LOCOMOTIVE COLLECTION

The Scottish Railway Preservation Society's collection is regarded by many as Scotland's national collection, and it also represents one of the major collections in the United Kingdom. On site are some 42 locomotives, 50 coaches and 76 wagons with a strong Scottish content. However, English-built examples are included, especially if they were used in Scotland – such as the LNER locomotive *Morayshire* built in Darlington. Two of the most interesting locomotives are North British Railway No. 673 *Maude* built by Neilsons in 1891, and Caledonian Railway No. 419 built at the St Rollox Works of the Caledonian Railway in 1907.

A recent arrival at Bo'ness from the Glasgow Museum of Transport is another North British Railway locomotive, No. 256 *Glen Douglas* built in 1913, which the Society hopes to restore to working order.

In addition to representing the operating railway companies, the locomotives also represent the products of a once great railway manufacturing industry in Scotland. Most of the companies declined as the age of steam drew to a close, but Andrew Barclay & Co. of Kilmarnock continued to export steam locomotives long after they had been withdrawn by British Railways. Barclays also produced very successful diesel locomotives, especially the smaller shunting engines for industrial use. There are several Barclay locomotives at Bo'ness – both steam and diesel. The North British Locomotive Company is represented by a diesel-hydraulic shunting locomotive.

When setting up a national collection the nostalgic appeal of the steam locomotive must be kept in perspective, and examples of other types preserved. There are now several main line diesel locomotives in the collection at Bo'ness, and also several small industrial electric locomotives suitable only for static display.

COACHES, WAGONS AND OTHER ITEMS

The coach collection includes examples of the various operating companies in Scotland over the years. The earliest, and most prestigious, is the 1897 Great North of Scotland Railway saloon which was used in King Edward VII's royal train. Another early coach was one built in 1901 for the Glasgow and South Western Railway.

Of particular interest is the collection of freight rolling stock with wagons, vans, hoppers, tank wagons and brake vans. Some of these were built in the 19th century, and many more in the first two decades of the 20th century. Their loads represented many of the industries of Scotland: coal, grain, parcels, steel, fish, chemicals and gunpowder.

An unusual group of rolling stock came from railway engineering departments, including several cranes, with one 36-ton steam breakdown crane built in 1914. A comprehensive collection of signalling equipment has been collected – some to

Approaching Bo'ness station on the Bo'ness and Kinneil railway on the train hauled by the replica of Robert Stephenson's Rocket. (Upper)

Caledonian Railway 0-4-4T No. 419 running round its train at Bo'ness Station. (Lower)

use on the operational line, but much to illustrate the history of signalling.

Having achieved their first objective of setting up a vintage railway, the Scottish Railway Preservation Society are now intent on improving their facilities. Parts of the collection are stored in large sheds to which the public do not normally have access, but can be seen by appointment. Plans are now being made to erect new buildings to enable the collection to be displayed and to be used to tell the story of Scotland's railways.

BONNINGTON MILL, WATERWHEEL

Bonnington Road, City of Edinburgh

View from road

Bonnington Mill was one of a series of water-using industrial units on the Water of Leith in Edinburgh. It was one of the last to use water power, but was derelict by the 1960s and was demolished in the late 1970s to make way for private housing. The cast-iron waterwheel latterly used probably dates from the re-equipment of the mill by Alex Mather &

Sons of Edinburgh in the early years of this century. It has been preserved on a plinth as a reminder of the history of the site.

BUCHAN'S POTTERY, KILNS

Portobello, City of Edinburgh

View from the street

These kilns are the last of their kind in Scotland, and are the sole upstanding remains of what was once a notable industry in the area. They were scheduled as monuments of national importance in the 1970s, so that when the owners, A. & W. Buchan, moved their business to Crieff in the later 1970s it was possible to secure their preservation. The upper part of the eastern kiln was rebuilt at that time. The kilns are now preserved by the local authority. Some of the machinery was preserved by the National Museums of Scotland, and Edinburgh City Museums have a good collection of products.

The waterwheel at Bonnington Mill, City of Edinburgh, salvaged when the mill itself was demolished.

The last two traditional pottery kilns in Scotland, at the site of Buchan's Pottery, Portobello.

BUTE MUSEUM

Stuart Street, Rothesay, Isle of Bute, Argyll & Bute
Tel: c/o Miss A. A. Montgomery (Hon. Sec.)
(01700) 502248

Open: *April to September every day (Sunday p.m.)*

October to March, Tuesday to Saturday (p.m.)

Admission: *Charges*

Refreshments: *None*

Parking: *Car park*

Disabled access: *Good, toilet nearby*

Bute's little museum sits tucked behind Rothesay's great ruined circular castle. It has the dignity of a purpose-built building, and the distinction of a long history of voluntary support. Its collections illustrate the natural history, history and archaeology of the island of Bute. There is not much of industrial interest, but one noteworthy item is a sheet-iron horn, said to have been blown to rouse the workers in the Rothesay cotton mills, the first of which was founded in the late 18th century to pirate Richard Arkwright's spinning patents.

Because Bute is an island, water transport is most significant. For many years Rothesay was a popular holiday destination for Glaswegians taking a steamer trip 'doon the watter'. In the history gallery of the museum there is a display of miniature models depicting Clyde steamers and ferries. Surviving artifacts include the ornate paddle-box crest from the *Duchess of Fife* and items of tableware from another of the steamers. The museum also has a very good photographic collection covering: yachts, puffers, paddle steamers, turbine steamers and the modern diesel ferries.

At the end of the 19th century, Rothesay had horse-drawn trams which were later replaced by electric tramcars. Small artifacts are preserved together with a photographic record. The museum makes good use of its resources by mounting temporary exhibitions of interest to locals and visitors alike.

The iron horn in the Bute Museum.

CALEDONIAN RAILWAY, BRECHIN

2 Park Road, Brechin, Angus

Tel: (01356) 622992

Talking Timetable or

(01674) 810318 Enquiries

Open: *Sundays, June to September*

Admission: *Free, charge for train journey*

Refreshments: *None*

Parking: *Car parks at both stations*

Disabled access: *Ramps at both stations, toilet at Brechin*

The Brechin Railway Preservation Society was founded in 1979 and in 1983 they purchased the former British Rail branch line from Bridge of Dun to Brechin. After many years of hard work the line was re-opened to the public, operated by the enthusiastic volunteers. From the Victorian station at Brechin the train journey covers a distance of about 4 miles (6.4 km) and terminates at Bridge of Dun Station which was formerly a junction on the Strathmore Line from Forfar. Nearby is Montrose Basin, a large tidal lagoon which is now a bird sanctuary.

The Victorian station at Brechin which is now the base of an operating vintage railway: Caledonian Railway, Brechin.

RAILWAY COLLECTION

Although the collection of locomotives is relatively small in numbers, it does have considerable variety. There are three small saddle tank locomotives, two built by Andrew Barclay of Kilmarnock in 1897 and 1926, and the other by Peckett and Sons of Bristol in 1915. Three World War II 'Austerity' locomotives and an LMS Ivatt Class 2 of 1950 complete the steam collection. Diesel locomotives are also represented by several shunters from the 1950s and three main-line locomotives from around 1960: a Class 20, a Class 26 and a Class 27. Not all of the locomotives are in service, as the volunteers are in the process of restoring a number of them.

CAMPBELTOWN MUSEUM

Hall Street, Campbeltown, Argyll & Bute

Tel: (01586) 552366, Ext. 2237

Open: *Monday to Saturday*

Admission: *Free*

Refreshments: *None*

Parking: *Nearby*

Disabled access: *Difficult (stairs)*

Campbeltown is situated at the southern end of the Kintyre peninsula and is about 60 miles (96 km) as the crow flies from Glasgow, but over twice

that distance by road. Transport by sea and later by air had certain advantages for freight and passengers respectively. A regular airline service from Glasgow to Campbeltown started in 1933 using an airfield at nearby Machrihanish. A light railway linked Machrihanish with Campbeltown and several small items from this railway are preserved in the museum.

The museum is housed in the Campbeltown Public Library and features local history including maritime items. There are several ship models including the SS *Kintyre* of 1868, and a number of half-models of ships associated with Campbeltown. Of particular interest is the collection of four lifeboat models starting with Campbeltown's first lifeboat the *Princess Alice* of 1860 to 1868. In addition, a collection of paintings illustrate a variety of ships, from fishing boats to a revenue cutter. Eight of the paintings show steamers operated by the Campbeltown Steam Packet Company.

Industrial exhibits include a model steam engine made in 1910 representing the engine used at a local lint mill, and a model of the steam engine which supplied power to the dried grains factory of the Campbeltown Distillers' Association until 1917. The Argyll Colliery at Machrihanish is illustrated by photographs, and the illicit whisky business is represented by a model still.

CAMPS VIADUCT

**Almondell Country Park,
East Calder, West Lothian**

View from footpath

Hidden in the valley of the River Almond, Camps was built in 1885 to carry a freight-only railway to Pumpherston shale-oil works. This closed in the 1960s and the viaduct then deteriorated. As it is located in Almondell Country Park, West Lothian District Council co-ordinated a repair scheme which has restored it to good condition and allows visitors to walk over it. Nearby is a unique cast-iron aqueduct carrying water from the river to the Edinburgh and Glasgow Union Canal. It was constructed in 1818–20 by the canal company and is built of wedge-shaped sections, so that although it looks like a bowstring bridge it is in fact an arched structure. It is also designed to metric, rather than imperial dimensions.

Camps Viaduct, Almondell Country Park, West Lothian, now in local authority care. (Below left)

Catcraig Limekilns on the seashore near Dunbar (Below)

C

CATCRAIG LIMEKILNS

Near Dunbar, East Lothian

View from footpath

Lime burning has been practised in Scotland wherever seams of limestone outcrop. The lime industry of the Lothians was particularly important, the lime produced being used both for agricultural improvement and for building. The sea-shore kilns at Catcraig used locally-quarried limestone and probably coal shipped from the Forth Estuary. They were restored in the 1960s by East Lothian County Council whose successors still maintain them.

CAWDOR CASTLE

Nairn, Highland
Tel: (01667) 404615
Fax: (01667) 404674

Open: *May to September*

Admission: *Charges*

Refreshments: *Restaurant*

Parking: *Car park*

Disabled access: *Limited, toilet*

A castle linked to the Thane of Cawdor of Shakespeare's *Macbeth* is not an obvious choice for a visit by students of industry and transport. However, castles and country houses often contain surprises due to the interests of their various occupants over the years.

Several members of the Cawdor family served in the Royal Navy and one of these was John Campbell who was a Lord of the Admiralty in 1741. It is probable that he acquired the very fine model of HMS *Victory* on display at Cawdor. This is not Nelson's *Victory*, but an earlier 100-gun warship, built in 1737, which served as the flagship of Admiral Sir John Balchen. The large model is built to a scale of 1/48 and is of particular interest because it is a dockyard model, which was made as a

guide to the shipwrights working on the construction of the actual ship at Portsmouth. Unfortunately, this *Victory* was lost with all hands in a storm off the Channel Islands in 1744. Another member of the Cawdor family served as Captain on Nelson's *Victory*. Sir Thomas Masterman Hardy survived a dangerous life at sea, but in his later life refused to travel by train because he considered it a 'needless risk'.

Over one of the castle windows is the nameplate of a Great Western Railway steam locomotive *Earl Cawdor*. This is not too surprising, as the 3rd Earl was Company Chairman. When the locomotive was withdrawn from service the present Earl purchased it and gave it as a Christmas present to his father, who is reported to have responded 'How very useful'. Incidentally, the *Room Notes*, written by Lord Cawdor, are full of irreverent and humorous comments – which make refreshing reading compared with many similar publications.

There is a small collection of cycles, a boneshaker *c*.1865, an ordinary (penny farthing) *c*.1880, and a tricycle which was nicknamed 'The Royal Mail' because it was 'swift and reliable'. Also on display is a small fire-engine *c*.1860, a dustcart, a Victorian pony sleigh, and for use by the head gamekeeper in winter – a pair of snowshoes.

CHARLESTOWN LIMEKILNS

Charlestown, Fife

View from road

Scotland's largest bank of limekilns, built by successive Earls of Elgin to burn limestone from adjacent thick seams. The harbour built for lime and coal shipment was greatly expanded in the late 19th century. Lime burning ceased in the 1930s, but the site operated as a lime depot until the 1960s. It lay derelict for some years, and was then tidied up using Manpower Services Commission labour. A scheme to develop the area as a low-key visitor attraction, with harbour and routes to the lime quarry, has not yet been implemented, but the kilns and harbour may be viewed from the road.

The limekilns at Charlestown, Fife, are the largest group in Scotland. (Upper)

Christies' Woollen Mill, Islay with the ancient piecing machine on the left. (Lower)

CHRISTIES' WOOLLEN MILL
(ISLAY WOOLLEN MILL)

Bridgend, Islay, Argyll & Bute
Tel: (01496) 810563

Open: *Monday to Saturday, 10am to 5pm*

Admission: *Charges*

Refreshments: *None*

Parking: *Limited*

Disabled access: *Limited*

One of the few surviving country woollen mills in Scotland, this factory was operated by the Christie family until the 1970s. In it all the processes of woollen cloth manufacture were carried out using machinery dating from the mid 19th century. The mill has the most remarkable collection of early spinning machinery in Scotland. It still produces tweed, though the spinning and carding machines no longer operate. It has the only piecing machine in Scotland, used to prepare carded fibre for spinning.

The horizontal mill at Dounby is the last survivor of its type in Orkney.

CLICK MILL, DOUNBY

Dounby, Orkney
Tel: None

Open: *All reasonable hours*

Admission: *Free*

Refreshments: *None*

Parking: *Limited*

Disabled access: *Difficult*

The horizontal or norse mill is one of the oldest types of powered grain mill, and as it requires no gearing is particularly suitable for areas with no ready access to specialist craftsmen. The power of a horizontal mill is, however, limited, so by the later 19th century they only survived in Scotland in the north and west Highlands and Islands. By the 1930s the Dounby Mill was the last in Orkney and because of its rarity was taken into the care of the Secretary of State. Consolidation work followed which straightened out some of the characteristic and picturesque irregularities in construction. The mill is one of the larger examples of its type, with the small single pair of stones at one end. Internally it gives a very vivid impression of the spartan simplicity of rural life in Orkney in the 19th century.

CLYDEBANK MUSEUM

Clydebank, Dunbarton & Clydebank
Tel: (01389) 737000

Open: *Mondays, Wednesdays and Saturdays*

Admission: *Free*

Refreshments: *None*

Parking: *On street*

Disabled access: *Yes*

Clydebank is known to the world for shipbuilding, birthplace as it was of the Cunard Queens, the world's largest liners, of great warships like HMS *Hood* and *Vanguard,* and of the Royal yacht *Britannia.* But Clydebank was very nearly named Kilbowie, and Kilbowie had the world's largest sewing machine factory, belonging to Singers, with the world's largest clock. The Clydebank Museum, situated in the town's central library, naturally focuses on this heritage of ships and sewing machines, with models of several Clydebank-built vessels and an unrivalled collection of sewing machines.

COMET REPLICA, PORT GLASGOW

Port Glasgow, Inverclyde

View from street

This full-scale working replica was commissioned by Lithgows Ltd. to commemorate the 150th anniversary of the first voyage of the craft, which was the first commercially successful steamboat in Europe. The original ship was devised by Henry Bell, with engine and boiler made in Glasgow and hull in Port Glasgow. The replica made a few trips under steam in 1962, the anniversary year, and then lay until the 1970s in Lithgows' yard. It now forms a striking feature in a waterfront car park.

CULZEAN CASTLE, GAS HOUSE

Culzean Castle, by Maybole, South Ayrshire
Tel: (01655) 770269

Open: *April to October, daily*

Admission: *Part of charge for country park*

Refreshments: *At visitor centre*

Parking: *Large car and coach park for country park*

Disabled access: *Difficult*

Many of the larger country houses in Scotland, particularly in the Lowlands, had small gas works to supply gas for lighting the house and neighbouring estate buildings. At Culzean the retort house and pit for the gasholder have survived, the latter buried under rubbish, and the former used as a studio by art students. The National Trust for Scotland has restored the retort house, rebuilt the chimney, exposed the gasholder pit and inserted an interpretive display, including replica retort ends. It opened to the public, as part of the interpretation of the Castle and grounds, in 1993. In the castle there are many ship models, mainly of yachts.

The replica of the Comet, the first commercially-operated steamboat in Europe, was built in 1962 for the centenary of its introduction.

DALAVICH, FOREST TRAIL

(see entry at **Glen Nant, Forest Trail**)

DALGARVEN MILL

Near Dalry, North Ayrshire
Tel: (01294) 552448

Open: *All year, daily*

Admission: *Charges*

Refreshments: *Coffee room*

Parking: *Car park*

Disabled access: *Limited*

This large Ayrshire water mill was operated as a provender mill until *c.*1970 then lay disused until revived as a visitor centre during the late 1980s. Restored waterwheel, country life displays and, traditional livestock make this an attractive facility.

Dalgarven Mill, near Dalry, North Ayrshire, typical in scale of the larger Ayrshire grain mills, is now a country life museum and visitor centre.

DALLAS DHU DISTILLERY

By Forres, Moray
Tel: (01506) 825855

Open: *All year*

Admission: *Charges*

Refreshments: *Dram or coffee after tour*

Parking: *Large car and coach park*

Disabled access: *To ground floor, not to upper levels*

Dallas Dhu is a Highland malt whisky distillery. It was built in 1898–9 by Wright & Greig, a Glasgow firm of whisky blenders whose prime blend was Roderick Dhu, hence the 'Dhu' in the distillery name. The architect was C. C. Doig, the leading distillery designer of his day, and although there have inevitably been some alterations to the buildings, they remain largely as constructed. The distillery is on an E plan, with the longest arm consisting of a malt barn. This has a barley loft on the first floor, and a malting floor on the ground floor. Part of the malting floor has been converted to a visitor centre, with shop/display and audio visuals room with bar for serving samples of whisky.

At right-angles to the malt barn is the pagoda-roofed kiln, used for drying the malt, and next to it

Part of the reception area at Dallas Dhu Distillery, showing a cooper's workshop, where barrels for maturing whisky are repaired. (Above)

Dallas Dhu Distillery, near Forres, Moray, one of the distilleries built during the 1890s whisky boom and designed by Elgin architect C. C. Doig. (Left)

the malt deposit, with malt mill below. Through a wall from the mill is the mash tun, where the crushed malt was mixed with hot water to extract sugars. Next to the mash house, and forming the middle arm of the E, is the tun room with six wooden wash backs in which the sugary liquid was fermented before distillation.

After fermentation, the wash was pumped into the stillhouse, where it was distilled twice, first in the wash still, then in the spirit still to produce new-make spirit, which was collected in the receiver room in an oak receiver. From that vessel the spirit was pumped into a larger oak vat in the filling store, in the remaining arm of the E, where the spirit was run into oak casks for maturing. Across the open side of the E are the bonded warehouses, where the barrels of maturing spirit are stacked. A viewing space has been formed where visitors can see the long rows of casks, and smell the heady aroma of the warehouse.

Dallas Dhu was sold by Wright and Greig in 1919, and eventually acquired by Scottish Malt Distillers, a subsidiary of the giant Distillers Company Limited, in 1930. It closed in 1983, as a part of a programme of reducing capacity in the industry, and in 1986 it was acquired on behalf of the nation by Historic Scotland, who adapted it for public access and opened it to the public in 1988. The aim has been to keep the distillery as far as possible as it was at closure, with Victorian buildings and equipment of the period 1938–1960. As time goes by, and other malt whisky distilleries change, or close, Dallas Dhu becomes more important as an historical document, and more fun to visit.

DALMELLINGTON AND DISTRICT CONSERVATION TRUST

Waterside, Patna, East Ayrshire
Tel: (01292) 531144

Open: *Daily in summer months*

Admission: *Charges*

Refreshments: *Buffet car*

Parking: *Car and coach park*

Disabled access: *To most of site*

In the upper reaches of Ayrshire's Doon Valley, made famous by Robert Burns, lies the parish of Dalmellington. This is on the route from Ayr into Galloway via Carsphairn, but was distinctly a backwater until the later 1840s when the completion of the leasing of Lanarkshire ironstone and coal pushed ironmasters into Ayrshire. The Houldsworth family, owners of Coltness Ironworks, of the Anderston Foundry and the Anderston Cotton Works in Glasgow, leased minerals in the neighbourhood of Dalmellington, and to smelt the ironstone built a new ironworks between Patna and Dalmellington villages. To serve it, a railway from Ayr to Dalmellington was promoted, but not completed until 1856. The Dalmellington Iron

The repair workshop at Dalmellington Ironworks, built in the 1840s, and recently restored by building industry trainees.

Company also built its own system of mineral railways to link the ironworks with the ironstone and coal pits serving it and with its clay hill. The ironworks eventually closed in 1921, and was dismantled, but the coal pits continued to operate, and in 1930 became part of Bairds and Dalmellington. They in turn built a brickworks on the site of the iron furnaces and chemical plant. Nationalisation of the coal industry in 1947 was followed by the driving of the Minnivey mine, the last new colliery in the Doon Valley, opened in 1956. Deep mining of coal was gradually reduced until in 1978 the last pit, Pennyvenie Nos 2 and 7, closed.

It was about this time that local interest in the history of the upper Doon Valley began to surface. Because the area had not been a focus for large-scale industrialisation after the ironworking period, nor for urbanisation, it became increasingly clear that the remains of 19th-century industrialisation were uniquely complete. With the demolition of ironworks remains at Muirkirk and Shotts, the importance of the furnace bank and engine house at Waterside became critical, and the other buildings of the ironworks period – workshops, offices and later power station and fan-engine house – were of complementary significance. The remains of the upland mining villages, such as Corbie Craigs, Benwhat and Lethanhill, and of the railways linking them to the ironworks put the finishing touches to an industrial landscape of remarkable – indeed national – importance.

This recognition led to the formation of the Dalmellington and District Conservation Trust in 1983, with the objectives of establishing an open-air museum at the ironworks, and of conserving and interpreting other aspects of the history of the village and parish of Dalmellington. The first practical expression of this was the conversion by Cumnock and Doon Valley District Council, with grant aid from the Countryside Commission for Scotland, of a row of weavers' cottages in Dalmellington into a visitor centre. This has been a focus for the development of the wider work of the Trust, and contains at the time of writing a re-creation of a handloom weaving shop, and material relating to the industrial history of the valley. More recently the centre of gravity of operations has

moved from Dalmellington to the ironworks site at Waterside, where the Trust's offices are now in a former laboratory building. The brick kilns, blowing engine house and workshops have been restored, and other buildings on the site are being rehabilitated. The intention of the Trust is to combine museum and interpretative use with craft workshops. Exhibits in store include a large number of small items: a haulage engine from the Sorn mine, made by Beckett & Anderson of Glasgow; a Weir steam pump from Highhouse Colliery; a steam crane; man-riding cars; a cage; and some wooden wagons from a rope-worked clay-mine railway at Dalry.

Complementing the work of the Trust is that of the Ayrshire Railway Preservation Group, who have established a Scottish Industrial Railway Centre at the site of the Minnivey mine. Here one can see products of Andrew Barclay, Sons & Co. Ltd. of Kilmarnock, including a fireless locomotive and a large diesel locomotive, and a number of wooden wagons, probably Scottish-built. There are in addition both standard and narrow-gauge locomotives and wagons that worked in a range of Scottish industries, including chemical manufacture, whisky blending and coal mining. A remarkable steam crane, with totally enclosed motion, worked in the rolling-mill roll works of R. B. Tennent & Co. at Whiffet. The ARPG has plans to operate train services from the Minnivey site to Waterside from the summer of 1996, and in the other direction track exists up to the site of Pennyvenie Nos 2 and 7 Colliery.

The 'Waterside Experience' also includes a pair of cottages in Chapel Row, Waterside, one of which has been furnished in the style of an ironworker's cottage of about 1920. The whole development is still in its relatively early stages, but there is much potential for creating an unusual industrial museum to celebrate the history of a beautiful and distinctive valley, illustrating the impact of industrialisation on a rural area.

General view of the former Dalmellington Ironworks, later adapted to a brickworks and now the centrepiece of the Doon Valley experience. (Above)

Equipment from the Stow College Laboratories, Glasgow, awaiting display in the workshop building at Dalmellington. (Below)

DAVID LIVINGSTONE CENTRE

Blantyre, South Lanarkshire
Tel: (01698) 823140

Open: *All year, every day*

Admission: *Charges*

Refreshments: *Tea room*

Parking: *Car and coach park*

Disabled access: *Fair*

David Livingstone was an explorer and Christian missionary of the Victorian period whose African journeys were of great importance in scientific, religious and political terms. He was born in the cotton mill village of Blantyre, where Henry Monteith, a Glasgow merchant, had established a cotton spinning, weaving and printing complex in the late 18th century. Livingstone worked as a boy in the spinning mills before studying at Anderson's College in Glasgow for the medical qualification which allowed him to become a missionary. His memorial is part of the row of cottages in which he was born and brought up, precious now not only for their connection with this remarkable man, but also as survivals of cotton mill housing in the west of

Scotland. Internally these houses have been much altered, but they do contain a full-sized section of a self-acting spinning mule, specially made by Platt Brothers of Oldham, and photographs of the once-powerful mill complex as well as displays on Livingstone and his life. Down the hill the bow-ended counting house survives, as does the great curved weir that channelled the waters of the Clyde into the mills, but neither forms part of the centre.

DENNY SHIP MODEL EXPERIMENT TANK

Dumbarton, Dunbarton & Clydebank
Tel: (01389) 763444

Open: *All year, except Sundays*

Admission: *Charges*

Refreshments: *Small tea room*

Parking: *Car park*

Disabled access: *Difficult*

This is one of Scotland's most remarkable industrial buildings, both in terms of its structure and contents and of its historical significance. It was built in 1882–4, at a time when shipbuilding was a very competitive industry, in terms of performance of ships, as well as in cost. William Denny & Bros. with a shipyard somewhat confined in the dimensions of the ships it could build, had already begun to specialise in high-performance passenger vessels, and secured orders by promising high speeds. Failure to meet specifications could result in serious financial penalties, or even in refusal to accept the ship. Dennys were therefore much taken with William Froude's method of using experiments with accurately-made models, towed in a tank, to predict the behaviour of a full-sized hull. This had been used for naval vessels during the 1870s, with success. William Denny in discussion with Froude agreed to build a ship model experiment tank which

The moving carriage to which models are attached for experimental purposes in the Denny Ship Model Experiment Tank, Dumbarton.

was the first in the world designed for merchant ship design. As built, it had a carriage moved by a rope attached to a steam engine, and had a cutting machine for transferring the lines from the design drawing to the wax model hull rough-cast in a clay mould. The tank itself was 300 feet long, with a brick superstructure. It was later extended by 30 feet.

The tank proved very successful, and Dennys maintained a high reputation for small, fast passenger vessels until the market for these dwindled in the later 1950s. The Denny yard closed in 1961, but the tank was taken over by Vickers Ltd., who continued to use it, latterly as part of British Shipbuilders, until the early 1980s. As a result of a remarkable combined initiative the tank was acquired from British Shipbuilders and assigned to the Scottish Maritime Museum. It is now run on a day-to-day basis by the SMM; with financial support from Dumbarton District Council, and under the guidance of a management committee with representatives from those agencies which contributed to the acquisition. It is now open to the public on a regular basis. When British Shipbuilders sold the tank, there was a clause in the agreement preventing the use of the tank for commercial work. During 1990 this restriction was removed.

More than a hundred years after it was built, the Denny Ship Model Experiment Tank is still largely in original condition. Additions have been made at the office and workshop end; electric propulsion has replaced steam, and instrumentation has been transformed. The models are still cast in clay moulds in cast-iron tanks, and the lines cut on the original machine. The principles of tank testing are unchanged. One of the most remarkable features of the tank is the complete set of test data from the very first model in 1884.

In the grounds of the tank is the little side-lever engine of the paddle steamer *Leven*, which was owned by the Dumbarton Steamship Company. The engine was built by Robert Napier, a Dumbarton man, and sat for many years below the castle rock at Dumbarton, and for a time in the shopping centre. It is a very fine example of an early paddle-steamer engine, dating from 1824.

DEVON COLLIERY, ENGINE HOUSE

Near Alloa, Clackmannanshire

View from park

Now set in a country park, this engine house, finely constructed of sandstone ashlar, still has the beam, and a section of pump-rod, of a steam pumping engine of the Cornish type. The engine was built by Neilson & Co. of Glasgow in 1865. When the area around the house was landscaped, the building was put into good order, and it has recently been converted to offices.

The pumping engine house at Devon Colliery, near Alloa, Clackmannanshire, showing the beam and pump rod.

DICK INSTITUTE

Kilmarnock, East Ayrshire

Tel: (01563) 526401

Open: *All year, except Sundays*

Admission: *Free*

Refreshments: *None*

Parking: *Car park*

Disabled access: *Limited*

The Dick brothers, founders of this institute, were Victorian entrepreneurs who exploited the market for belts for driving machinery, using then new natural products, gutta percha and balata. In the beginning they very successfully made shoes with gutta percha soles ('gutties') anticipating the almost universal use today of leather substitutes. They were natives of Kilmarnock and built the institute as a gift to their birthplace. The institute contains a library as well as a museum.

The industrial component of the displays relates to Kilmarnock's engineering industry, which grew up to serve the local coal pits and ironworks, and developed an international reputation for industrial locomotives, pit winding engines, and for a brief period tramcars.

DISCOVERY (ROYAL RESEARCH SHIP)

Discovery Point, Discovery Quay, Dundee City

Tel: (01382) 201245

Fax: (01382) 225891

Open: *Daily*

Admission: *Charges*

Refreshments: *Café*

Parking: *Car park*

Disabled: *Access to Discovery Point and main deck of Discovery; toilet*

The Royal Research Ship *Discovery* was the first ship to be designed and built specifically for scientific research and Antarctic exploration. She was built in Dundee where many robust whaling ships had been constructed in the past, and launched on 21 March 1901. Later in the year, Commander (later Captain) Robert Falcon Scott and his crew left for the Antarctic. For two years the *Discovery* was trapped in the ice but returned home safely in 1904. She was sold in 1905 and for his ill-fated expedition of 1910 Scott sailed in another Dundee-built ship, the converted whaler *Terra Nova*.

Following her Antarctic expedition the *Discovery* had a very long and varied career including transporting munitions to Russia during the 1914–1918 War, and taking part in several scientific expeditions. The British, Australian and New Zealand Antarctic Research Expeditions of 1929 to 1931 were notable on several counts for not only did they carry out valuable scientific work under appalling conditions, but also their work was recorded by photographs and cine-film. The intrepid photographer, Frank Hurley, took his pictures hanging precariously from the rigging in heavy seas, and from the air in a de Havilland *Gipsy Moth* biplane which was carried on board the *Discovery*. Hurley's film *Siege of the South* is a classic.

From the 1930s, *Discovery* served as a training ship and was not subjected to major alterations; consequently, her layout today is very much as the sailors and scientists of the 1929–1931 expeditions knew her. She was rescued from the breakers yard in the late 1970s by the Maritime Trust who restored her, and opened her to the public at St Katherine's Dock, London. Then, in 1986, *Discovery* returned to Dundee on board a massive transporter ship and is now in the care of the Dundee Heritage Trust. Much careful restoration work has been carried out.

The historic ship is now moored at Discovery Quay between two of Dundee's landmarks – the road and rail bridges across the River Tay. At Discovery Point there is an excellent sequence of exhibits which prepares visitors for their tour of the ship using theatrical sets, models, films, videos, graphics, music and animation. Of particular interest are the plans of the ship, the huge model of the Panmure Yard where she was built, and the launching ceremony. The story of the 1901–1904 expedition is covered by several presentations including a 13-minute show *Locked in the Ice*.

On board *Discovery*, visitors can tour the deck and study the reconstructed masts and rigging. Although the ship had a steam engine powered by coal-fired boilers, she normally relied upon her sails, as only a limited amount of coal could be carried. The original 450 hp triple-expansion steam engine made by Gourlay Bros of Dundee, has not survived but an excellent reproduction engine has been fitted complete with sound effects.

The tour of the ship includes all the facilities reconstructed as they were for the expeditions of 1929 to 1931 under Sir Douglas Mawson – even to the sheep loaded at Cape Town to provide fresh meat.

DISTILLERIES

Apart from **Dallas Dhu** Distillery, Forres, preserved as a monument in the care of the Secretary of State, and the museum at **Glenkinchie** (both with separate entries), there are many distilleries in Scotland which are open for visits by the public. The facilities for visitors vary widely, but most incorporate some historic artifacts and most of the distilleries themselves have some historic fabric.

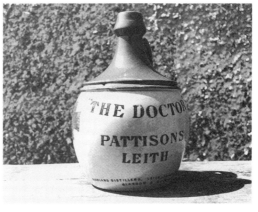

The Royal Research Ship Discovery, built in Dundee in 1901 and now a tourist attraction at Discovery Point between the two Tay bridges. (Upper)

A whisky jar made for Pattison Bros., a short-lived Edinburgh firm of blenders, in the 1890s, now in the Museum of Islay Life, Port Charlotte. (Lower)

Current information on which distilleries are open to the public may readily be had from Scottish Tourist Board publications, or from the Scotch Whisky Association.

DOUNE MOTOR MUSEUM

Doune, Perthshire & Kinross
Tel: (01786) 841203
Fax: (01786) 841203

Open: *April to October*

Admission: *Charges*

Refreshments: *Café*

Parking: *Car park*

Disabled access: *Access and facilities good*

A 1938 Bugatti Type 57C at the Doune Motor Museum. (Upper)

A Rolls-Royce Phantom II Continental of 1935, one of Doune's many cars in running order. (Lower)

Each of the half dozen motor museums in Scotland has a completely different character. The collection of cars at Doune represents the top of the range, displayed in immaculate condition and usually in running order. It was built up by the Earl of Moray, initially as a small collection for his own use and enjoyment, starting in 1953 with a 1934 Type 26 Hispano Suiza. Several high-performance cars followed and in 1968 the Doune Hill Climb Course was opened. This course consists of about a mile (1.6 km) of winding up-hill road on the Doune Estate, up which cars compete for the fastest timed run. This attracted motor enthusiasts to Doune and generated an interest in the collection of cars. Farm buildings adjacent to the Hill Climb Course were converted into a museum which opened in 1970.

In addition to three Hill Climb weekends, many other motoring events make use of the Doune Motor Museum: car rallies, motorcycle rallies, an autojumble and so on. As most of the cars in the collection are kept in running order they may be seen out and about being driven by their enthusiastic owner, or displayed at special events, or competing at vintage race meetings.

The Doune collection of about 50 cars does not have any particular theme, nor does it attempt to demonstrate the technical history of the motor car. It does not include anything but high quality cars (and six motorcycles) covering the period from 1905 to the 1970s.

Pride of place goes to a 1905 Rolls-Royce, owned by the Royal Scottish Automobile Club, which is the second oldest Rolls-Royce car in the world and the only surviving example of one with a three-cylinder engine. In fact, it was built before the Rolls-Royce

company was founded in 1906, but it was built by Rolls and sold by Royce. At the other end of the scale are two Ferraris of 1973, a *Daytona* and a *Dino*. Most of the famous marques are represented from Alfa Romeo to Volvo.

Each car is a star in its own right, often with an interesting life story. The descriptive labels and guide book make fascinating reading – especially for anyone remotely interested in cars. One such story concerns a 1913 three-litre Sunbeam racing car bought for a young man who lived in Galloway. Unfortunately, he was killed in the 1914–1918 War and his mother ordered that the Sunbeam should be buried. Many years later it was discovered by a farm worker while ploughing a field. It was recovered and restored – a poignant reminder of one lost racing driver.

The Earl of Moray's interest in racing and high-performance cars is represented in the collection. These were (and still are) driven in hill-climb events. Scottish-built racing cars are few and far between, but one displayed at Doune is the JP Special of 1958. This small racer with a 500 cc engine was designed by Joseph Potts at a time when Formula 500 was extremely popular and gave many famous drivers, such as Stirling Moss, a start in motor racing.

The cream of the collection are, however, the quality cars: Aston Martin (4), Bentley (5), Jaguar (4) and Rolls-Royce (4).

DOUNREAY NUCLEAR EXPERIMENTAL ESTABLISHMENT, EXHIBITION CENTRE

Reay, Caithness, Highland
Tel: (01847) 802121 ext. 2702

Open: *Mid May to mid September, Tuesday to Sunday*

Admission: *Free*

Refreshments: *Yes*

Parking: *Car park*

Dounreay Nuclear Experimental Establishment has been a prominent feature of the Caithness landscape since its establishment in the 1950s. Among the work carried out here were studies on nuclear reactors for ship propulsion and on fast-breeder reactors. An exhibition centre has been opened to explain the work of the establishment, and there are tours of the Prototype Fast Reactor.

DUMFRIES AND GALLOWAY AVIATION MUSEUM

Heathhall Industrial Estate, Dumfries,
Dumfries & Galloway
Tel: None at Museum. Contact (01387) 259546 evenings

Open: *Weekends, Easter to October*

Admission: *Charges*

Refreshments: *None*

Parking: *Car park*

Disabled access: *Most display areas accessible*

Facilities: *Toilet accessible*

Scotland has two aviation museums which both occupy sites on World War II airfields, but otherwise they are completely different, which means that both are worthy of a visit. The **Museum of Flight** at East Fortune is a conventional museum run by the National Museums of Scotland whereas the Dumfries and Galloway Aviation Museum is run by a group of enthusiastic volunteers. Members of the Dumfries and Galloway Aviation Group started their operations by recovering items from aircraft crash sites throughout south-west Scotland and northern England. The interest in aviation

Behind the wing of the De Havilland Vampire is the North American F-100D Super Sabre supersonic fighter at the Dumfries and Galloway Aviation Museum.

archaeology grew very rapidly during the 1970s and involved its devotees in some very difficult and back-breaking work. Aircraft tended to crash in inaccessible regions such as lochs, mountains and bogs; the latter often provided better protection for the surviving parts, but made recovery difficult. The recovered parts, such as engines, undercarriages, structural components and instruments, had to be cleaned and treated to avoid further corrosion. Members of the group also researched the details of the crashed aircraft and its crew. This work provided useful back-up for displays by providing some fascinating stories.

The museum was opened in July 1977 in the control tower of RAF Dumfries. The building also needed digging out as it had been used for many years by a farmer to house his animals. The displays feature the story of the airfield and local aviation history in general.

To supplement the remains of crashed aircraft the group set out to acquire a limited number of complete aircraft commencing with a de Havilland *Vampire* jet trainer in 1976. They now have five jets and a Bristol *Sycamore* helicopter. All but the *Vampire* are the only examples of the type on display in Scotland and pride of place goes to the North American F-100D *Super Sabre* – the first aircraft to enter service which was capable of supersonic speeds in level flight. Another interesting foreign jet fighter is the French Dassault *Mystere* IV of 1952. In addition to the complete aircraft, there are several fuselage sections which include the cockpit. Visitors are allowed to sit in several of the cockpits and enjoy a real 'hands-on' experience.

Of the relics recovered from the archaeological digs, aero engines tend to survive in one piece and these are featured on the ground floor of the control tower. The first floor displays tell the more human-interest stories with records, photographs and uniforms. One wreck recovery display is still under preparation. An early *Spitfire* Mark II crashed in Loch Doon on 25 October 1941 and there it remained until 1982 when it was located and raised. Restoration work on the recovered parts is a time-consuming task which is being tackled by the enthusiastic volunteers of the Dumfries and Galloway Aviation Group.

DUMFRIES MUSEUM

The Observatory, Dumfries, Dumfries & Galloway
Tel: (01387) 253374
Fax: (01387) 265081

Open: *April to September, every day; October to March, Tuesday to Saturday*

Admission: *Museum free; Camera Obscura – charges*

Refreshments; *None*

Parking: *Car park*

Disabled access: *To Museum but not to Camera Obscura; toilet*

One of the museum buildings is a local landmark which can be seen from quite a distance as it was a windmill, built in the 18th century. When threatened with demolition, the tower was saved by a public appeal in 1834 and converted into an observatory. Two years later a camera obscura was installed to view the surrounding town and countryside and this is still operating.

The tower of an 18th century windmill converted into a camera obscura and now part of Dumfries Museum.

Like many early museums, the collections consisted of rarities and oddities, but the remit of the museum today is to present the history, natural history and geology of the Dumfries and Galloway Region. Local industries are represented by the tools and implements of the farmer, saddler, joiner and blacksmith. The size of the museum precludes large industrial or transport objects. There is a small collection of bicycles including an early copy of Kirkpatrick Macmillan's first pedal bicycle *c.*1840 (*see also* **Scottish Cycle Museum**). This copy was made by an apprentice wheelwright who saw Macmillan's machine some years earlier.

In the town there is a full-size replica of William Symington's first steamboat built in 1788 for Patrick Miller of Dalswinton. This was tested on Dalswinton Loch about 6 miles (11 km) north of Dumfries with several well-known passengers on board including Robert Burns, and the artist Alexander Nasmyth who painted the scene. Symington's small steam engine was a Newcomen-type (atmospheric engine) and this is preserved at the Science Museum in London. Symington's third steamboat, the *Charlotte Dundas* is widely recognised as the first practical steamboat (see **Falkirk Museums**).

DUNDEE ART GALLERIES AND MUSEUMS

McManus Galleries, Albert Square, Dundee City (Broughty Castle Museum, Broughty Ferry, Dundee City)
Tel: (01382) 432020
Fax: (01382) 432052

Open: *Monday to Saturday*

Admission: *Free*

Refreshments: *Nearby*

Parking: *Public car park nearby*

Disabled access: *Access and facilities good*

Dundee Art Galleries and Museums has four branches, of which the McManus Galleries building in the city centre is the largest. This Gothic building was designed by Sir George Gilbert Scott in 1867. The permanent displays cover the history of Dundee from prehistoric settlement to the modern day. These include an exhibition telling the story of Dundee's trade and industry from the medieval burgh to the 1960s, and a separate display on life in the city in the 19th and 20th centuries. The rest of the building has permanent art and decorative art displays, and hosts temporary exhibitions. There are also related displays in the branch museum at Broughty Castle, 6 miles (9.5 km) east of Dundee city centre. The Castle is an 1860 Victorian coastal fort and access to the displays is by internal stairs.

INDUSTRIES

To many youngsters the most important products of industrial Dundee must be the *Dandy* and *Beano* comics, which are published by D. C. Thomson & Co. Ltd., whose headquarters are just across the square from the museum. However, historians would probably give pride of place to the linen and jute industries, followed by engineering, shipbuilding, docks, the manufacture of jam and marmalade, and the once important whaling industry. All of these industries are dealt with in the Trade and Industry Gallery at the McManus Galleries, where paintings, photographs, Trades Union banners, models and tools are displayed. In addition, more detailed displays covering the local fishing and whaling industries are located at Broughty Castle. Dundee had the largest whaling fleet in Britain in the last quarter of the 19th century and many of these robust vessels were built in Dundee, as was Commander (later Captain) Scott's *Discovery* now on display at Discovery Quay.

The industrial displays at McManus Galleries do not dwell entirely on the past, as the modern improvements in the docks and the postwar diversification away from textiles are also featured.

ROAD TRANSPORT

There are no motor vehicles on display although the museum does own a Daimler double-decker bus which was registered with Dundee Corporation in 1951 and is kept in the reserve collection. On display at the McManus Galleries are two road vehicles from the 1930s – an ice-cream seller's tricycle and a parcel delivery barrow.

RAIL TRANSPORT

The story of the tragic 1879 Tay Bridge Disaster is told in the Trade and Industry Gallery with graphic illustrations and some poignant reminders, such as a contemporary collage of tickets collected from the ill-fated passengers at the station before the bridge. Contemporary models and plans of the bridge are also shown. In the same gallery there are a number of very good models on display to represent some of the early local railways, such as the *Earl of Airlie* of 1833 from the Dundee Newtyle Railway. The *Kinnaird* of 1847 depicts the next generation of larger locomotives; this one was designed by the famous engineer Thomas Crampton for the Dundee and Perth Railway.

AVIATION

Although the collection includes some models of aircraft and archives, these are not on display. The models include examples of the unusual aircraft designed by a local pioneer Preston A. Watson. He built three aircraft between 1908 and 1913 which incorporated a rocking wing as a means of control. Some short flights were achieved, but the idea was ingenious rather than practical.

MARITIME

The maritime displays in the Trade and Industry gallery at the McManus Galleries include many ship models, paintings and contemporary illustrations depicting the story of sea-borne trade to and from Dundee and the traditions of Dundee ship-building from wooden sailing-ships to large oil-tankers.

Also on display is one of the oldest boats in the country; this is a Pictish log-boat, dating from around AD 500, which was found in the River Tay in the 19th century. It is 26 feet (7.90 m) long and remarkably intact. Another very significant maritime item is the earliest surviving dated example in the world of a mariner's astrolabe, an instrument used to navigate by sighting the positions of the sun and stars. It was made in 1555 by the Portuguese instrument maker and cartographer, Lopo Honem. On its reverse side is stamped 'ANDREW SMYTON 1688' – Smyton was a Dundee shipmaster in the 1680s.

Tickets collected from passengers killed in the Tay Bridge disaster of 1879 and now in Dundee Museum. (Upper)

A Pictish log-boat built in the 1st century and found in the 19th, also in Dundee Museum. (Lower)

At Broughty Castle there are displays on the history of the fishing community of Broughty Ferry, and on the local lifeboat service. There is also a gallery telling the story of Dundee's whaling fleet including ship models, crewmen's souvenirs and whaling tools from one of the most significant collections in Britain. On display in the first-floor gallery there is a model of the train-ferry crossing from Broughty Ferry to Tayport which operated up until the building of the first Tay Rail Bridge.

DUNFERMLINE MUSEUM

Dunfermline, Fife
Tel: (01383) 721814

Open: *All year*

Admission: *Free*

Refreshments: *None*

Parking: *Pay car park*

Disabled access: *Limited*

The linen trade is in popular imagination often linked to Ireland, but its history in Scotland is probably as long, and almost as distinguished. The origins of linen manufacture in Scotland go back deep into the early history of settlement, as flax was the only fibre-bearing plant well adapted to the Scottish climate. It is comparatively easy to make coarse brown yarn and hence cloth, and such cloth was durable and strong. To make finer cloth, and whiter, involves a high level of skill, and the process of making white linens was developed on the Continent, especially in Holland, in the 17th century. Linen and woollen manufacture were both encouraged by the Scottish government before 1707, but after that date the pre-eminent woollen trade of England swamped the nascent one of Scotland, so far as more sophisticated cloths were concerned. To redress the balance, the United Kingdom Parliament in 1726 set up a body to stimulate the development of industry, especially the linen trade. The so-called Board of Trustees for Improving Fisheries and Manufactures of Scotland encouraged linen manufacture by offering prizes to raise quality and premiums to stimulate investment, and by importing foreign expertise. This took time to take effect, but by the later 18th century the linen industry was becoming significant, and had begun to generate its own innovations, especially in bleaching, an adjunct to the fine linen trade. As much of the raw material used – flax – was imported, especially from Russia, the east coast became particularly associated with this trade, especially with the coarse end. Fine linen became a west of Scotland speciality, a role it retained until cotton ousted it. In the east, Fife and

Perthshire remained strongholds of finer linen production, and after the invention of the Jacquard loom, Dunfermline, Perth and to a lesser extent Kirkcaldy became noted for damask weaving, in which a self-coloured fabric has a pattern woven into it detectable by changes in texture. Dunfermline became pre-eminent, and during the 1920s and 1930s silk weaving was grafted onto the linen tradition. The Dunfermline Museum has a room devoted to the local textile trades, with two looms, a Jacquard card-punching machine, and cases in which changing displays of small objects, including samples of textiles, are mounted. The museum also possesses collections of railway archives and of cycles.

A damask loom on display in Dunfermline Museum. The weaving of linen and silk damask cloth was a speciality of the town.

EDRADOUR DISTILLERY

Near Pitlochry, Perthshire & Kinross
Tel: (01796) 472095

Open: *March to October, Monday to Saturday*

Admission: *Free*

Refreshments: *At end of tour*

Parking: *Car and coach park*

Disabled access: *Limited*

Edradour is Scotland's smallest licensed malt whisky distillery. It is the last of the small distilleries which were founded under the provisions of the 1823 Excise Act, and though it has been modernised, most recently to accommodate visitors, it retains much of the character of small-scale distillation. All the main features of a malt whisky distillery are there, though the interior of the malt barn has become a visitor reception area, and malt is now brought in crushed, ready for mashing. The tiny mash tun, wash backs and uniquely small stills are all in the same building, as was once common, and one piece of equipment, a Morton's refrigerator (used for cooling the malt liquor before fermentation) is now the only one of its kind still in use. One can regret the loss of the home-made character of the distillery as it was until the early 1980s, but in general the adaptations necessary to permit large numbers to visit it have been well and thoughtfully carried out.

The main production buildings at Edradour Distillery.

ELGIN MUSEUM

1 High Street, Elgin, Moray
Tel: (01343) 543675

Open: *Monday to Saturday, all day; Sunday p.m.*

Admission: *Charges*

Refreshments: *Nearby*

Parking: *Public car park nearby*

Disabled access: *Ramps, toilet*

The Elgin and Morayshire Literary and Scientific Association was founded in 1836 by local antiquarians and naturalists. By 1843 they were able to open one of the first purpose-built museums in Scotland. The Association later became The Moray Society who still administer the museum. The museum's principal collections cover archaeology and geology; however, there are displays of local industry and some interesting transport items.

One of the earliest transport exhibits is a log-boat, or dugout canoe, probably dating from the Iron Age. This was excavated from the banks of the River Spey over 100 years ago. Another early form of river transport is a coracle, or curragh, also used on the River Spey. This leather-covered wicker boat dates from the late 1700s and is the only surviving one in Scotland. As well as being used for transport and salmon fishing, curraghs were used to guide logs down the River Spey from the forests of Abernethy to the coast. Some of the timber was then used in the local shipyard at Kingston-on-Spey, while the rest was shipped to other parts of Scotland and even abroad. The museum has several models of boats built locally including a 'Zulu' fishing boat and a schooner.

There are a number of items relating to turnpikes and stage-coaches, including a Bill listing the passengers and parcels carried by the Elgin Star Light Post Coach from Elgin to Inverness on 23 May 1827. More picturesque is an inn sign from the *Royal Oak* dating from *c.*1815. The museum has an interesting archive and photographic collection covering roads, railways and shipping.

A Souter diesel engine in Elgin Museum, a rare example of a Scottish-made single-cylinder engine of this type.

Barn machinery in Falkirk Museum Workshop. (Upper)

Probably the only surviving caravan of its type, built in 1939 by Thomson's Coachworks, Falkirk and now in the Falkirk Museum Workshop. (Lower)

FALKIRK MUSEUMS

(Grangemouth Museum, Kinneil Museum, Museum Workshop, Callendar House, etc.)
c/o Falkirk District Museums, Kilns House, Kilns Road, Falkirk
Tel: (01324) 624911
Fax: (01324) 614026

Open: *Confirm by telephone*

Admission: *Free (except Callendar House)*

Refreshments: *None*

Parking: *All sites have a car park*

Disabled access: *Access and facilities good except: Kinneil Museum, limited; Grangemouth Museum, not suitable*

MUSEUM WORKSHOP (OPEN STORE), GRANGEMOUTH

As with so many of Scotland's industrial museums and collections, this one had its origins in the availability of Community Programme assistance to museums in the early 1980s. This allowed Falkirk Museums to put together, and in some instances to conserve and restore, a wide range of objects relating to industry in the district. These are now stored in an industrial unit, which is open to the public during July and

August and occasionally at other times. The 'open store' treatment is remarkably effective, the unexpected juxtaposition of objects drawn from different industries and periods producing effects which are sometimes startling and always interesting. One should, I suppose, wish for a 'proper' museum display for many of the exhibits, but formalising their exhibition would be a loss, too. It is refreshing to see a collection with so little formal interpretation, and one which therefore gives scope to the imagination. Items in the collection include steam engines and other prime movers, foundry equipment and products (notably grates and ranges, in which the district specialised), farm machinery, machine tools, and clay mining and processing equipment.

Most of the transport collection is housed at the Museum Workshop in Grangemouth. As the name implies, this is an active workshop with restoration work being carried out on some of the objects. A major project of recent years has been the restoration to running order of a 1931 Falkirk tramcar; this single-deck Brush Pullman tram was found locally during 1979 serving as a garden shed and, after many years of work, is now nearing completion.

Also on display are: a Fowler diesel shunting locomotive from the local British Aluminium works, a travelling crane c.1940, three tractors and a 1911 motor plough, a mobile threshing machine and bothy, and a most unusual caravan. This ultra-lightweight camping trailer was built by Thomson's Coachworks of Falkirk in 1939 and is probably the only surviving example.

GRANGEMOUTH MUSEUM

The Grangemouth Museum was refurbished in 1993 to tell the story of one of Scotland's earliest planned industrial towns. Its story is linked to the Forth and Clyde Canal built in 1790, with its eastern terminus at Grangemouth. Also featured are the steam boat experiments of William Symington which took place on the canal. Symington's first small steam boat was tested on Dalswinton Loch in Dumfriesshire; his second was tested on the Forth and Clyde Canal using an engine made by the local Carron Company. His third, and most successful

paddle steamer was the *Charlotte Dundas* using a horizontal steam engine, again built by the Carron Company. This vessel proved its practicability by towing two barges for almost 20 miles (32 km) on the Canal in March 1803. *Charlotte Dundas* is widely accepted as the world's first practical steam boat – but she was not preserved. During the 1980s the Falkirk Museum Service set about the task of building a working replica of *Charlotte Dundas*. This was a major undertaking for a small museum: the hull has been built and work on the engine is in progress.

FIFE FOLK MUSEUM

The Weigh House, Ceres, Cupar, Fife KY15 5NF

Tel: (01334) 828250

Open: *Easter, mid May to October, (afternoons). Closed Fridays. Other times by appointment*

Admission: *Charges*

Refreshments: *None*

Parking: *Public car park nearby*

Disabled access: *Access to most areas. Steep ramp to garden*

Fife Folk Museum is run by a voluntary organisation, the Fife Folk Museum Trust, and the quality of their work has resulted in several awards. The museum was opened in 1968, in the 17th-century Tolbooth and Weigh House plus an adjoining 18th-century cottage. Another cottage and gardens were added shortly afterwards and, in 1984, a site opposite the museum became available and an extension was built.

Local industries and crafts are described with the aid of tools and equipment used by the farmer, thatcher, blacksmith and farrier, stonemason, joiner-cartwright, tinsmith, cobbler, linen weaver, brewer and clay-pipe maker. Appropriately for a former Weigh House, there is a good display of weights and measures, scales and balances, including iron beam-scales found in the rubble when the derelict building was being restored. Many of the other items were made by the firm of John White & Son, founded in the early 18th century and still in business in Fife.

Transport exhibits include a small display on turnpikes including a local Toll board. There is also a pony trap dating from the early 1900s and used at Hill of Tarvit (a nearby National Trust for Scotland mansionhouse). A small collection of early bicycles includes a hybrid between a hobby-horse and a Kirkpatrick Macmillan crank-driven machine, and also a 'boneshaker'.

FORDYCE, JOINER'S SHOP

Fordyce, Aberdeenshire

Tel: None

Open: *Easter to October, daily*

Admission: *Free*

Refreshments: *None*

Parking: *Car park nearby*

Disabled access: *Yes*

The joiner's shop was a very characteristic feature of villages throughout Scotland. Apart from building work, joiners were also undertakers, and made coffins as required. This important rural craft has now been commemorated in the opening of this typical workshop in the picturesque village of Fordyce. Its pantiled roof is characteristic of east-coast building, and the multipaned windows, with small panes overlapped without horizontal glazing bars, are entirely typical of such buildings throughout Scotland.

The joiner's shop at Fordyce, Aberdeenshire, typical of such buildings, which were once very common in country villages.

GAIRLOCH HERITAGE MUSEUM

Auchtercairn, Gairloch, Highland

Tel: (01445) 712287

Open: April to September Monday to Saturday; October to March, by prior arrangement

Admission: Charges

Refreshments: Restaurant adjacent

Parking: Car park

Disabled access: Access and facilities good

This museum is easily found because outside there are two boats and a lighthouse lantern. It is run by the volunteers of the Gairloch and District Heritage Society and housed in an attractively restored farm steading. The aim is 'to explain and interpret the past life in the Parish of Gairloch', according to the guidebook. This is not as modest as it sounds because the parish is extensive, and has, or had, many diverse activities within its boundaries – including a major naval base at Loch Ewe during the 1939–1945 war. The guidebook is well worth reading for it gives the background to, and significance of, the principal exhibits.

Several local industries are covered, including agriculture – the museum itself was the steading for Auchtercairn Farm, and the restaurant was the byre. In addition to arable farming, sheep were reared on the higher ground and the displays feature the related cottage industries of spinning, weaving and knitting – the area was famous for 'Gairloch Stockings'. Fishing, using small boats such as the two on display, provided food for local people and fish were also salted for export to the Baltic, Ireland and Spain. The still-active peat industry is clearly explained, and there is an example of an apparatus which used peat as fuel – the illicit whisky still. An industry not widely associated with the Highlands was iron smelting, but the shortage of wood for charcoal in England in the late 16th century resulted in Scottish iron-ore deposits being developed. On display are some documents and a lump of iron slag from one of the local furnaces near Loch Maree.

Transport in the Parish was very dependent on the sea with Poolewe on Loch Ewe as the main port. The lighthouse lantern and fog horn on display came from Rudha Reidh Lighthouse on the approach to the entrance of Loch Ewe. Also on display is a model of the small steamer *Mabel*, which carried passengers along Loch Maree before World War I. The museum has a good collection of archive material and photographs to support its displays.

GLASSAUGH WINDMILL

Near Sandend, Aberdeenshire

View from the road

Known locally as the 'cup and saucer' this is the stump of a tower windmill used for grinding grain. It has recently been conserved by a local trust. The platform which surrounds the tapering tower, and which gives the structure its nickname, was used for setting the sails on the mill.

Glassaugh Windmill, near Sandend, Aberdeenshire – locally known as the 'cup and saucer'.

GLENCOE AND NORTH LORN FOLK MUSEUM

Glencoe Village, Argyll & Bute
Tel: None

Open: *Mid May to September, Monday to Saturday*

Admission: *Charges*

Refreshments: *None*

Parking: *In street*

Disabled access: *Good*

Situated in the village of Glencoe, this voluntary museum is in two traditional buildings. Most of its displays are on folk life, but the local slate industry, the largest in Scotland, is also featured.

GLENKINCHIE DISTILLERY MUSEUM

Glenkinchie, near Pencaitland, East Lothian
Tel: (01875) 340451

Open: *All year, Monday to Friday (except Christmas and New Year)*

Admission: *Free*

Refreshments: *At end of distillery tour*

Parking: *At distillery*

Disabled access: *Poor*

Glenkinchie is one of the very few surviving Lowland malt whisky distilleries. It was rebuilt in the late 19th century in red and white brick, unusual materials for rural distillery buildings. In common with other distilleries in the Scottish Malt Distillers' empire, malting ceased here in 1968, and the disused malt barn provided an ideal place to receive items of historic distillery plant, collected by the manager with the blessing of SMD. After a period of technical stability lasting about 70 years, the malt whisky distilling trade moved forward rapidly during the 1960s and early 1970s, and the Glenkinchie collection is unique and irreplaceable.

The former cottages which house the main displays in the Glencoe and North Lorn Folk Museum. (Upper)

The stillhouse section of a 1:12 scale model malt whisky distillery, built for the 1924 Empire Exhibition at Wembley, and now in the Glenkinchie Distillery Museum. (Lower)

Pride of place must go to the superb large-scale model of a representative malt whisky distillery, built by Bassett-Lowke for the 1924 Wembley Exhibition. By virtue of its linear, opened-up layout, this is not only an important historical document but also an immediately accessible introduction to the principal elements in malt whisky distilling. There are many smaller exhibits, ranging from the implements used in malting to stillhouse relics, including rummager chains used to prevent local overheating in coal-fired stills. This is an extraordinarily rich and varied collection, and its display in juxtaposition to a working distillery in a building where some of the implements were used gives it an unusual degree of authenticity.

GLENLUCE MOTOR MUSEUM

North Street, Glenluce, Newton Stewart,
Dumfries & Galloway
Tel: (01581) 300534

General view of the display in the Glenluce Motor
Museum.

Open: *March to October (every day); November to
February (closed Monday and Tuesday)*

Admission: *Charges*

Refreshments: *Available*

Parking: *Car park*

Disabled: *Access and facilities good*

Glenluce is a small village about 10 miles (16 km) east of Stranraer, the ferry terminal for Northern Ireland. There are many attractions for tourists in this south-west corner of Scotland, but transport museums are few and far between. Although Glenluce has lost its railway, it does have a very impressive viaduct. The Glenluce Motor Museum is very much the creation of its owner Bill Adams, who has collected cars, motor cycles and motoring memorabilia for many years.

ROAD TRANSPORT COLLECTION

The collection consists of about a dozen cars and almost 20 motor cycles. As the collection was brought together on a very limited budget it does not contain the Bentleys and Bugattis; indeed, the dominating theme seems to be the small car starting with the Morris *Minor* of 1929, Austin *Seven* tourer of 1933 and a 1938 Standard *Eight*. From the 'bubble car' era of the 1950s there is a Messerschmitt and Isetta, and from the 1980s the ill-fated Sinclair C5. For those who are interested in rarities there is a 1925 Daimler, the only known example of its kind, and a 1967 Triumph TR4A *Dove Special*, one of only two built. The 1920 Snaith motor cycle built in Retford is another rarity and the Ariel of the same year is an interesting machine. Some of the vehicles are on loan, which results in changes to the displays from time to time.

Motoring memorabilia are displayed in every available space: costumes, petrol cans, horns, miniature cars, and many other items. An interesting feature is the replica garage workshop where restoration work in progress can be viewed. Although not exactly 'road transport' there is also an unusual collection of grass-cutting machines.

GLEN NANT, FOREST TRAIL

Taynuilt, Argyll & Bute

Tel: None

Open:	*All reasonable times*
Admission:	*Free*
Refreshments:	*None*
Parking:	*Car park*
Disabled access:	*Poor*

This trail, and another not far away at Dalavich on the west side of Loch Awe, have been laid out by the Forestry Commission to take the visitor through mixed forest areas that in the 18th and 19th centuries were worked to supply charcoal to the iron-smelting furnace at **Bonawe**. Trees were encouraged to grow several slender trunks (coppiced) which were then cut into short sections and burned to make charcoal on circular platforms formed on the hillsides. In this way the same forest could be regularly cropped. On both trails platforms can be seen laid out to show how the wood was built up into heaps for charring, and the routes used by pack horses taking the charcoal to the furnace may still in some instances be traced.

GOLLACHY, ICE HOUSE

Gollachy, near Portgordon, Aberdeenshire

Tel: None

Open:	*Reasonable hours*
Admission:	*Free*
Refreshments:	*None*
Parking:	*On road*
Disabled access:	*Reasonable*

Gollachy is a hamlet which in earlier times earned its living by fishing, using beach boats. The turf-roofed ice house stored ice for preserving fish in transit, and is an unusual variety – more orthodox specimens have obviously vaulted roofs and are set into banks. This one is cared for by Moray District Council and has an interpretation board.

GRAMPIAN TRANSPORT MUSEUM

Alford, Aberdeenshire

Tel: (019755) 62292

Fax: (019755) 62180

Open:	*April to October inclusive*
Admission:	*Charges*
Refreshments:	*Refreshment area*
Parking:	*Car park*
Disabled access:	*Access and facilities good*

Alford (pronounced A-ford) is situated some 27 miles (43 km) east of Aberdeen, and is not one of the most visited villages in Scotland, despite the

The 'Craigievar Express' steam car, now in the Grampian Transport Museum, seen here at Craigievar Castle.

A display of early cars in the Grampian Transport Museum.

fact that it boasts one of the best transport museums in the country. The Grampian Transport Museum is one of the modern breed of all-action museums. As one would expect, the main theme of the displays represents the history of land transport, with particular relevance to the north east of Scotland – a large snow plough, for instance.

There are about 100 vehicles, large and small, on display but these are not 'fixtures'. Most are in working order, while many are privately owned and lent to the museum for a year or two. Visitors are allowed to clamber over the more robust exhibits – such as the snow plough – and enjoy push-button exhibits and video displays. There is a re-created Wheelwright's Shop, a Garage Workshop, an exhibition on Roadmakers, and an adventure playground for the children. The museum can be far from quiet; in addition to the sound of children enjoying themselves there is a working organ. This 1923 Mortimer Dance Organ, made in Belgium, may have little to do with transport in Grampian, but it does entertain the visitors. A café scene also entertains with the sights and sounds of the swinging sixties.

Another unique feature of the museum is its racing circuit. Although not up to grand prix standard, this half-mile road circuit is used most weekends for Go Karting and special events. The latter include demonstration runs by a variety of vehicles, from vintage cars to modern racing machines. Competitions include a Moped Marathon and timed sprint events for a wide range of fast (and not so fast!) cars and motorcycles.

ROAD TRANSPORT

The changing collection of horse-drawn vehicles, cars, motorcycles and cycles on display attempts to keep a balance between old and new, popular and luxurious, large and small. Commercial vehicles are featured in an adjacent building capable of housing the huge Mack snow plough, a steam roller, a fire engine, etc. A double-decker bus doubles as a video cinema usually showing two separate presentations. In addition to an 1896 Aberdeen horse tram, the museum is restoring a unique electric tram which served the Cruden Bay Hotel. Visitors can view the work in progress on this tram.

Two steam-powered exhibits are major attractions. A Marshall portable steam engine named *Birkhall* was used on the Royal Estate at nearby Balmoral to power a saw-mill from 1942 to the 1970s. 'Portable' engines had wheels but had to be towed, as the steam engine was designed to be used only as a source of power to drive machinery. *Birkhall* was presented to the museum by His Royal Highness, the Duke of Edinburgh and was restored

to working order in 1992. The other steam exhibit is even more unusual. The *Craigievar Express* is a three-wheeled steam-powered road vehicle built in 1895 – before the first motor car arrived in the area. It was built by an ingenious postman called Andrew Lawson from Craigievar, which is just a few miles from Alford. Steam road vehicles were used with limited success during the 19th century, but few survive. The *Craigievar Express* was acquired in 1984 and is kept in working order for demonstration runs.

RAILWAYS

Just a short walk from the main museum is the Alford Valley Railway Museum (the admission ticket covers both museums). The displays of photographs and models are housed in the reconstructed station, originally built by the Great North of Scotland Railway in 1859. Alford was the terminus of the now-closed Alford Valley Line. However, working locomotives are to be seen on the narrow-gauge Alford Valley Railway. Both diesel and steam locomotives haul passenger trains from the station to two country parks. There is also a working model railway operating fine scale-model locomotives, which also haul passengers on some weekends.

Birkhall, a working portable steam engine from Balmoral, presented to the Grampian Transport Museum by HRH the Duke of Edinburgh.

HAWICK MUSEUM

Wilton Lodge, Hawick, Scottish Borders
Tel: (01450) 373457

Open: *April to September, daily; October to March,*
daily except Saturday and Sunday

Admission: *Charges*

Refreshments: *Café*

Parking: *Car park*

Disabled access: *Limited*

In most respects Wilton Lodge is a typical local museum, in an attractive but undistinguished house on the outskirts of Hawick. As Hawick is the capital of the Scottish knitwear industry one might expect some reference to that trade. What is unexpected is the large collection of knitting machines housed in one of the rooms, going back to hand-made stocking frames. In addition to these important but somewhat technically obscure devices, the museum houses some paintings of Hawick which show in a uniquely vivid way the transition of the town from a community of small manufacturers using hand techniques to a centre for large-scale manufacture.

The pithead gear and winding engine house at Highhouse Colliery, Auchinleck, preserved by the local authority after the colliery closed in the 1980s.

HIGHHOUSE COLLIERY, PITHEAD GEAR

Auchinleck, East Ayrshire

View from road

When Highhouse Colliery closed in 1983 it was the last Ayrshire pit with a steam winding engine, and the last with 'traditional' pithead gear. The headgear was in fact constructed in the late 1960s to replace a timber structure, but the engine and its brick house date from about 1896. Cumnock and Doon Valley District Council, to commemorate the significance of mining in the district, preserved these features when a small industrial estate was created on the site of the colliery, though the engine is no longer accessible.

HOPEMAN HARBOUR, CRANE

Hopeman, Moray

View from footpath

On a slope above the harbour is a little mobile hand crane, built by Cameron and Bowser of Glasgow in the late 19th century, which after many years of service in the harbour has been painted up as a monument. It is a particularly pleasing little crane, and one of very few such surviving.

A small mobile harbour crane, used at Hopeman, Moray, and now preserved there.

HUNTERSTON NUCLEAR POWER STATION, VISITOR CENTRE

Near Fairlie, North Ayrshire
Tel: (01800) 838557 (Freephone)

Open: *March to November, daily*

Admission: *Free*

Refreshments: *None*

Parking: *Car and coach park*

Disabled access: *Limited*

Hunterston A was the first nuclear power station in Scotland, and its magnox reactors provided base-load electricity from 1964. It is now being decommissioned, but survives unaltered externally. Hunterston B, an Advanced Gas Cooled Reactor Station, was completed in 1976, and is in full production. Scottish Nuclear, its owners, have opened a visitor centre and provide tours which, though primarily aimed at dispelling public fears about nuclear generation, offer the opportunity to see a recent but historic British technology at work. Trainees at Hunterston have been restoring a steam engine at **New Lanark**.

HYDRO-ELECTRIC VISITOR CENTRE, PITLOCHRY

Pitlochry, Perthshire & Kinross
Tel: (01796) 473152

Open: *Exterior viewing all reasonable times, Visitor Centre April to October, daily*

Admission: *Exterior viewing free, charge for Visitor Centre*

Refreshments: *None*

Parking: *Car parks on both sides of river*

Disabled access: *Limited*

The expansion of the hydro-electricity industry in the Highlands after the Second World War was an important and distinctive development. Its

Pitlochry dam and fish ladder, with the building housing the visitor centre on the left.

impact was dramatic, drawing rural communities into styles of living previously associated only with urban areas. The construction of the dams, water channels and power stations provided much work for Scottish engineering and building contractors. The most public face of all of this activity was the dam and power station at Pitlochry, on the river Tummel, where an interpretive centre was built, as well as a viewable fish ladder. These remain in place, now with a period flavour, as effective reminders of a most valuable and cost-effective investment in the Scottish economy.

INVERKEITHING MUSEUM

The Friary, Inverkeithing, Fife

Tel: (01383) 413344

Open: *All year, Wednesday to Sunday*

Admission: *Free*

Refreshments: *None*

Parking: *Street parking*

Disabled access: *Not suitable for wheelchairs*

Inverkeithing is one of Fife's ancient royal Burghs and its small museum is housed on the first floor of one of its old buildings, the Friary. The museum is one of three set up by the former Dunfermline District Council, the others being the Dunfermline Museum, and the Pittencrieff House Museum. The latter is a 17th-century mansion set in parkland, presented to the town by Andrew Carnegie, who was born in Dunfermline and later made a vast fortune in America (his birthplace is also a museum). The Pittencrieff House Museum features temporary exhibitions, but just outside there is a 1934 steam locomotive made by Andrew Barclay of Kilmarnock.

Inverkeithing is dominated by the Firth of Forth as it is situated at the northern end of both bridges, with Rosyth Naval Dockyard to the west and a shipbreaking yard to the east. The museum contains material covering all of these, including photographs and archives which can be seen by appointment. An earlier model of Rosyth Dockyard has recently been replaced by a new one, which is the centrepiece of the display covering the history of the Dockyard. Not many museums feature the industry of shipbreaking, but an exhibition tells the story of Ward's Shipbreaking Yard at Inverkeithing which has seen the demise of many famous ships.

INVERNESS MUSEUM AND ART GALLERY

Castle Wynd, Inverness, Highland

Tel: (01463) 237114

Fax: (01463) 712850

Open: *All year, Monday to Saturday and Sunday in July and August*

Admission: *Free*

Refreshments: *Coffee shop*

Parking: *Public car park nearby*

Disabled access: *Good, no toilet*

Like many of the museums in Scottish towns, the Inverness Museum had its origins in a learned society, in this case the Northern Institution for the Promotion of Science and Literature which was founded in 1825. The present museum building dates from 1966 and the general standard of the displays is very high.

On the ground floor there is a general transport theme, which shows how the Highlands have been 'opened up' by road, canal, rail and air. It begins with a display on General Wade's military roads built after the Jacobite uprising of 1715, and features a military engineer in his mobile office tent. Then follows a display on the roads and bridges built by Thomas Telford almost a century later. Telford designed his roads for stage-coaches and the objects in the display are from the coaching era – coach lamp, post horns etc. Telford was also involved in the building of the Caledonian Canal through the Great Glen from Fort William to Inverness, which was opened (unfinished) in 1822.

Longman Municipal Aerodrome, Inverness in 1937 featuring Capt. Fresson (in plus fours) with his Highland Airways aircraft and staff (Painting by Edmund Miller in Inverness Museum).

There is a small display on the canal, including a contemporary plan.

The coming of the railways in the mid 19th century was disastrous for many canals, but the Caledonian Canal did not have a railway line in direct competition. Several railway services to Inverness were opened in the 1850s, then the original companies were merged to form the Highland Railway in 1865. The display on the Highland Railway includes several model locomotives and a waiting room diorama.

Air travel came to the Highlands and Islands in the mid 1930s. There were two great rivals competing for passengers, especially on the services to Orkney and Shetland. Eric Leslie Gandar Dower's airline, Allied Airways, flew most of its services from Aberdeen, while Captain Ernest Edmund Fresson's Highland Airways operated most of its services from Inverness. There is a display on air travel and on Captain Fresson in particular, with some of his log books, first day airmail covers, and several personal items. The centre-piece of this display is a painting by Edmund Miller depicting a Highland Airways scene, entitled *A Flying Start to the Day*. The setting is Longman Municipal Aerodrome, Inverness in 1937. One of the aircraft in the background is a de Havilland *Dragon*, now preserved by the Science Museum, London on their airfield site at Wroughton, near Swindon.

An improvement in road travel has been the spectacular Kessock Bridge across the Beauly Firth which was opened in 1982, and this is covered by a display illustrating its construction.

Displays of trades and industry include a section on bagpipe manufacture, a taxidermy workshop (mounting stags' heads was once in great demand by shooting parties), and a reconstructed silversmith's shop – Inverness was noted for its silver in the early 19th century.

INVERVAR, GLEN LYON, LINT MILL

Invervar, Glen Lyon, Perthshire & Kinross
Tel: None

Open: *All reasonable hours*

Admission: *Free*

Refreshments: *None*

Parking: *On other side of road*

Disabled access: *Poor*

The linen industry in Scotland was encouraged after the Union of the Parliaments in 1707 by the United Kingdom government, which set up in 1726 the Board of Trustees for the Encouragement of Manufacturers and Fisheries in Scotland. Among other incentives, it offered grants towards the cost of establishing lint mills, for the preparation of flax for spinning, and bleachfields for finishing linen yarn and cloth. As a result, many small industrial units were established throughout the country, often in areas left behind by later industrial expansion. One such is the little lint mill at Invervar. This is a small circular building which had in it scutch mill machinery driven by a narrow overshot waterwheel, the site of which can still be seen. In this, locally grown flax, after steeping in a pond (retting) to rot the woody material connecting the fibres in the plant stem, was hammered by rotating wooden knives to remove the woody particles and soften the fibres. These could then be combed (heckled) to separate short fibres (tow) from long (dressed line), both of which could be separately spun into yarn. The lint mill at Invervar is the only circular example in the country, and one of only a handful of recognizable survivors. It was restored by Perth and Kinross District Council, who have put in interpretation, and who manage it as a monument.

IRVINE, GLASGOW VENNEL, FLAX-DRESSING SHOP

Irvine, North Ayrshire
Tel: (01294) 275059

Open: *June to September, daily except Wednesdays;*
October to May, Tuesdays and Thursday to Saturday

Admission: *Free*

Refreshments: *None*

Parking: *On street nearby*

Disabled access: *Good*

This little building is hallowed by association with the poet Robert Burns, who worked there for a brief period. Of the building within which Burns worked it is likely that only the walls survive, but the scale and setting give a valuable insight into the character of an important textile process. Here scutched flax from a lint mill (*see* **Invervar**) was heckled using iron-toothed combs to separate short fibres (tow) from long (dressed line), both of which would be spun into yarn on spinning wheels. It was hard, dusty work.

ISLE OF ARRAN HERITAGE MUSEUM

Brodick, Isle of Arran, North Ayrshire
Tel: (01770) 302636

Open: *May to September, Monday to Saturday*

Admission: *Charges*

Refreshments: *Tea room*

Parking: *Car park*

Disabled access: *Good*

The Isle of Arran Heritage Museum is a fine example of a voluntarily organised local museum. From our point of view its main interest is the well-preserved blacksmith's shop – 'smiddy' – which forms a part of the complex. This, with its bellows, hearth and complement of tools, is a worthy exemplar of the many country smiddies which provided ironwork, such as gate hinges, building components, and horseshoes, for agricultural communities throughout Scotland. The museum also displays a number of agricultural implements used on the island, mostly made by Scottish manufacturers.

The 'smiddy', Isle of Arran Heritage Museum, Brodick, a typical building of the type.

KEATHBANK MILL

Blairgowrie, Perthshire & Kinross

Tel: (01250) 872025

Open: *April to October, daily*

Admission: *Charges*

Refreshments: *Coffee shop*

Parking: *Car park*

Disabled access: *Yes*

The river Ericht, which flows through the centre of Blairgowrie, provided water power for a series of linen and jute mills sited on its banks. Because its flow was not always reliable in summer, these mills, as did many other country mills, installed supplementary steam engines. At Keathbank both the large waterwheel and the steam engine still exist. This is now the only mill in Scotland with its original steam and water-power equipment still in place, and in its form, scale and setting is a very fine example of a rural textile mill. The wheel, which is 5.5 m in diameter and 4.3 m in width, was built by J. Kerr of Dundee in 1865, and the engine was constructed by Carmichael & Co., also of Dundee. It is now managed as a visitor centre, with a model railway as part of its attractions.

The National Trust for Scotland's weaver's cottage in Kilbarchan, Renfrewshire, an early example of this type.

KILBARCHAN, WEAVER'S COTTAGE

Kilbarchan, Renfrewshire

Tel: (015057) 705588

Open: *June to August, daily; April, May, September, October, Tuesday, Thursday, Saturday, Sunday*

Admission: *Charges*

Refreshments: *None*

Parking: *Car park nearby*

Disabled access: *Limited*

Kilbarchan has been a weaving village since the early 18th century. At first, linen was the fabric woven, and the west of Scotland became renowned for its fine linens. From the 1780s, however, cotton began to oust linen, and in the 1820s a considerable expansion of handloom weaving took place in Kilbarchan, many of the village houses dating from that period. With the increasing sophistication and efficiency of power looms, that trade, too, declined in the later 19th century. Unlike many weaving villages, however, a few weavers switched to wool, and produced goods like travelling rugs, the last working until the 1950s. The National Trust for Scotland acquired the oldest (built 1723) and most picturesque of the cottages in 1957, and it has for many years been open to the public, with a loomshop in the semi-basement and domestic

accommodation in other rooms. Successive generations of local people have given artifacts to the cottage, so that it is now furnished rather more lavishly than it would have been, but it a very pleasing thing, and in the scale of the accommodation gives a very fair impression of a well-doing craftsman's style of living nearly three centuries ago.

Kinnaird Head Lighthouse, Fraserburgh, the first lighthouse lit by the Commissioners for Northern Lights, and now in the care of Historic Scotland.

KINNAIRD HEAD LIGHTHOUSE AND SCOTLAND'S LIGHTHOUSE MUSEUM

Fraserburgh, Aberdeenshire

Kinnaird Head was one of the first four lights established by the Commissioners for Northern

Lights. When first lit in 1786 its lantern was set on top of the 16th-century tower house. The engineer was Thomas Smith, whose son-in-law Robert Stevenson, in the late 1820s, rebuilt the light with a conventional tower inside the tower house. The lantern was replaced by one with triangular panes in 1849, and the optical apparatus was renewed in 1902. The foghorn, with its Glasgow-built diesel-powered air compressors, also survives intact. Kinnaird Head has been chosen as the Scottish lighthouse to be preserved with its traditional equipment, not only for its intrinsic interest, but also as a monument to the notable contributions to lighthouse design made by Scottish engineers. It has been taken into care by Historic Scotland, and was opened to the public in 1995, in association with a new Scottish National Lighthouse Museum created by the local authorities on an adjacent site. The new museum, designed by Morris & Steedman of Edinburgh, contains many relics of the lighthouse service, including optical apparatus from a number of lights, as well as smaller items and models.

KINNEIL MUSEUM AND KINNEIL HOUSE, BO'NESS

Bo'ness, Falkirk
Tel: (01324) 624911 ext. 2472

Open: *House may be viewed externally at all reasonable times. Museum: April to September, Monday to Saturday (June, July, August also Sunday); October to April, Saturday only*

Admission: *Free*

Refreshments: *None*

Parking: *At stables, limited*

Disabled access: *Limited*

Kinneil is an honoured name in Scottish industrial history, as it was in the 1760s the home of Dr John Roebuck, one of the founding partners of Carron Company, Scotland's first major ironworks. While at Kinneil, Roebuck employed James Watt to work on his steam engine, and the little building

James Watt's workshop at Kinneil House, with the Newcomen engine cylinder from the Schoolyard Pit on the left.

Watt used as a workshop still stands, roofless, behind Kinneil House. Beside it is a large Newcomen engine cylinder from an engine said to have been installed by Watt at the Schoolyard pit, worked by Roebuck to provide coal for Carron. Incidentally, Roebuck is credited with introducing long-wall working of coal into Scotland at the Kinneil pits.

The stables for Kinneil House, a little distant from it, were in a pleasing little vernacular building which was converted in the 1970s into a museum by Falkirk District Council. It houses displays on local history, including the Roebuck and Watt connections, and on the once-important Bo'ness Pottery, the latter including representative samples of its ware.

KIRKCALDY MUSEUM

Kirkcaldy, Fife

Tel: (01592) 260732

Open: *All year, daily except public holidays*

Admission: *Free*

Refreshments: *Tea-room*

Parking: *Car park*

Disabled access: *Fair*

Kirkcaldy is world-renowned for its linoleum industry, the first of its kind, but the town also made linen cloth (indeed still does), bricks and pottery, and there were nearby coal mines. These industries created the wealth that allowed the town's museum to be built in 1925, and are now reflected in its collections and displays. The linoleum industry is represented by tools and samples, and the pottery industry by a very fine collection of Wemyss Ware, a distinctive and attractive hand-painted product. Smaller displays illustrate other industries.

Leaderfoot Viaduct, near Melrose, Roxburghshire, the major engineering work on the Berwickshire Railway, opened in 1865.

LEADERFOOT VIADUCT

Near Melrose, Scottish Borders

View from road

Opened in 1865 by the Berwickshire Railway, Leaderfoot was the major engineering work on that agricultural line. The through route was severed in 1948 by the Border flood of that year, but the stub to Earlston, with the viaduct, carried freight until the 1960s when it succumbed to the Beeching cuts. Leaderfoot was identified in 1985 as one of a handful of outstanding disused viaducts, and has been repaired as a monument, with the deck waterproofed. It is expected that it will be opened to the public in 1998 by Historic Scotland, in whose care it will be.

LECHT, IRONSTONE MINE

Near Tomintoul, Aberdeenshire

View from footpath

Apart from spoil heaps, all that remains of iron and manganese mining in this elevated part of Scotland is a somewhat enigmatic building that may

have housed crushing or winding equipment, more probably the latter, and its associated water course. The relationship of the two makes it almost certain that a large waterwheel on one gable of the building had two sets of buckets, so that it could be made to revolve in either direction. Such wheels are otherwise only known from old engravings. This intriguing building is looked after by Kincardine and Deeside District Council.

This enigmatic building at the Lecht is the most substantial relic of the iron and manganese mining activity in the area.

LINLITHGOW UNION CANAL SOCIETY MUSEUM

Manse Road Basin, Linlithgow, West Lothian

Tel: (01506) 671215 or

c/o Mrs. Joy Galloway (01506) 842123

Open: *Weekends, Easter to September or by appointment*

Admission: *Free*

Refreshments: *Tea room*

Parking: *Car park*

Disabled access: *Access and facilities to the Museum good, no access to the boats*

The Union Canal, opened in 1822, linked the eastern end of the Forth and Clyde Canal with Edinburgh. This made canal travel possible between Glasgow and Edinburgh but, unfortunately, the advent of the railways in the 1840s made its success rather limited. Although passengers rapidly transferred to the railway, heavy goods such as coal and stone were carried by the canal until the early years of the 20th century. The canal was officially closed in 1965, but survived as a supply of industrial water for Edinburgh. During the 1960s and 1970s, a renewed interest in canals for leisure purposes led to the founding of the Linlithgow Union Canal Society. Volunteers spent many hours cleaning out the canal and setting up a museum. They also re-introduced passenger-carrying boats in order that visitors could enjoy travelling along this historic and scenic waterway, with the highlight of a trip across the River Avon on the spectacular Avon Aqueduct. One of the boats is a replica of a Victorian steam packet boat, while the other is a replica barge. Smaller boats are also available for hire.

CANAL MUSEUM

The museum is housed in a building which was once a canal stable, situated at one of the 'basins' along the canal where barges could moor while their horses were rested or changed. The basin was also used as a coal wharf. On display are photographs and small artifacts associated with the Union Canal together with a short audio-visual display. The aim of the museum is to show the development of the British canal system and explain the construction and working of the Union Canal in particular.

LIVINGSTON MILL

(see entry for **Almond Valley Heritage Centre**)

LOCHARBRIGGS SANDSTONE QUARRY, CRANE

Locharbriggs, Dumfriesshire

View from road

Sandstone has been quarried at Locharbriggs for well over a century, and the durable, warm red stone is still being used in building construction. Until the 1970s much equipment from Victorian times was still in use including a range of hand cranes in a dressing shop. One of these has now been painted in bright colours and stands as an advertisement at the entrance to the working quarry, which now uses advanced techniques for stone extraction and working.

LOCHORE MEADOWS COUNTRY PARK, PITHEAD GEAR

Lochore, Fife

View from park

When the Mary Colliery was dismantled, the concrete headgear (built in 1902) was retained as a monument to the once-important coalmining industry of the area. As a result of land reclamation it now sits in a country park, and it is complemented by a typical colliery 'pug' locomotive which gives scale to this unique concrete structure. A visitor centre has displays on land reclamation.

The concrete headgear from the dismantled Mary Colliery, now in the Lochore Country Park, with a colliery 'pug' engine giving an indication of its scale. (Above)

A vertical steam engine by Marshall of Gainsborough, in the gasworks at Hamilton and now preserved in the museum there. (Below)

LOW PARKS MUSEUM

Hamilton, South Lanarkshire
Tel: (01698) 283981

Open: *All year, daily, except Sunday*

Admission: *Free*

Refreshments: *None*

Parking: *Car park*

Disabled access: *Limited*

The museum of Hamilton is in the former office of the Duke of Hamilton's Estate there, a fine two-storey Georgian building. Among the displays are three of industrial interest. In the late 18th and early 19th century Hamilton was noted for hand-loom weaving, fine hand spinning and lace making, and on show are some woven fabrics and lace. The other noted local industry was coalmining, and there is a room devoted to models and small artifacts representing it. Of full-sized machinery there are two examples, both steam engines, from the local gasworks. One, by Waller of Stroud, drove an exhauster to draw gas out of the retorts, and the other, by Marshall of Gainsborough, was a vertical driving engine. The museum is currently being reorganised.

LOWTHERS LIGHT RAILWAY

Leadhills, South Lanarkshire
Tel: None

Contact: *C. Munro, High Barbeth, Leswalt, Stranraer, Wigtownshire*

Open: *Weekends; Easter, May to September*

Admission: *Charges*

Refreshments: *None*

Parking: *Limited*

Disabled access: *Limited*

The Lowthers Light Railway is constructed on the track bed of the Leadhills and Wanlockhead Light Railway. This was built under the Light

Rolling stock on the Lowthers Light Railway, seen at Leadhills Station.

The Worthington-Simpson steam pumps at Lyness.

Railway and Tramway Act of 1896, opened in1901, and closed in 1939. The Lowthers line has been constructed by enthusiasts, and is a two-foot gauge railway running from the site of Leadhills Station towards Wanlockhead. Its present terminus is at Glengonnar mine, one of the largest of the lead mines for which the area is famous.

LYNESS OIL PUMPING STATION, HOY

Scapa Flow Visitor Centre, Lyness, Hoy, Orkney

Tel: (01856) 791 300

Open: *Monday to Friday, 9am to 4.30pm, October to May; daily, June to September*

Admission: *Charges*

Refreshments: *Tea room*

Parking: *Car and coach park*

Disabled access: *Good*

When Britain began to prepare in earnest for the possibility of a Second World War, it became necessary to re-establish Scapa Flow as a northern base for capital ships and their attendant warships. By that time, oil fuel was universally used in the Royal Navy, and so massive oil storage capacity was needed. A tank farm was constructed, and a steam pumping station built to take oil from a jetty (where tankers could discharge) to the storage tanks. Steam power was used so that the boilers could also supply steam to heat the oil in the tanks to make it liquid enough to pump. The equipment consisted of four triple-expansion Worthington–Simpson non-rotary pumps with Lancashire boilers and supporting condensers, air pumps and feed pumps. During the war, storage capacity was increased by constructing underground tanks at a higher level. To serve these a diesel-powered pumping station (not open to the public) was built. When the Ministry of Defence closed the Lyness facility in the early 1980s, Orkney Islands Council acquired the site, and demolished most of the tank farm. They decided, however, to preserve one of the tanks and the pumping station. Round these fixed items a range of other objects have been accumulated, including a steam crane from the boom defence yard at Lyness, guns salvaged from warships in Scapa Flow, and some railway material from various sources, including the Royal Naval Armaments Depot at Crombie on the River Forth. The pumping station and tank, both scheduled ancient monuments, are open to the public as a Scapa Flow visitor centre.

MCLEAN MUSEUM, GREENOCK

15 Kelly Street, Greenock, Inverclyde

Tel: (01475) 723741

Open: *All year, daily, except Sundays*

Admission: *Free*

Refreshments: *Café*

Parking: *On streets nearby*

Disabled access: *Good*

The McLean Museum was founded in 1876 by Mr James McLean, a native of Greenock. It sits behind the rather grand Watt Library, erected in 1837 at the expense of James Watt's son, and is now the local history and reference library for Inverclyde District. The museum is somewhat overshadowed by its neighbour. Recently refurbished, it has been transformed from a typical Victorian museum into an attractive and well-laid-out modern museum, with well-chosen objects handsomely displayed and labelled in an informative but not over-wordy way. The main hall in the museum is a galleried rectangle, which traditionally housed exhibits relating to the maritime history of Greenock and Port Glasgow. In the new displays the ground floor has been laid out to illustrate the industrial and transport history of these communities, which dominate Inverclyde district. Shipbuilding, marine engineering, rope and cord making, sugar refining, pottery and whaling all feature, as do Clyde steamers. Some of the exhibits are of national importance, reflecting the significance of Greenock and Port Glasgow in Scotland's industrial history.

Greenock's most famous citizen, James Watt, is represented by a case of artifacts including two of his copying presses and a brace and set of bits. Next to this are two panels of samples from the Gourock Ropeworks, the largest rope-making concern in the world. Sugar refining is represented by models of 19th-century and mid-20th-century crystallising pans, and of a sugar-cube making machine. The 19th-century pan model is an excellent representation of an innovative machine. Two cases of products and moulds illustrate the Clyde Pottery's quality and refinement, one of the most interesting objects being a decorated wash hand basin, similar to two installed in the museum.

The maritime exhibits not surprisingly dominate the display. Half-hull builder's models of three of the greatest China tea clippers, the *Aeriel*, *Taeping* and *Lahloo*, all built in Robert Steele's yard, are probably the most important, but there are fine models of the *Clan Sutherland* (Greenock Dockyard Co.), *Mona's Isle* and Bell's *Comet*, also good amateur-built models of a revenue cutter and of a yacht under construction. The crafts of shipbuilding are represented by pneumatic caulking and riveting hammers and by a rivet hearth.

Marine engineering was a notable Greenock industry. The greatest of the early firms, Caird & Co., built trunk engines to drive screw steamships, and there is a splendid large model of one. Two fine coloured drawings of side-level paddle engines illustrate earlier products of the firm. The output of John G. Kincaid, last of the Greenock marine engineers, is represented by a large-scale model of a slow-speed diesel engine of Harland & Wolff /Burmeister & Wain type.

John Hastie & Co. were renowned for steering-gear manufacture, and there are models of two types of screw steering gear, and of a Hele–Shaw pump, as built by the firm for hydraulic steering gear.

Two full-sized exhibits are of particular interest. Outside is a small vertical steam engine from one of the Greenock shipyards, a rare specimen of a once common type. The other is the governor of the waterwheel of the Greenock Cotton Mill, a unique survival, and notable because the 70 foot (21.4 m) wheel was the largest of its kind in Scotland.

MELROSE MOTOR MUSEUM

Abbey Road, Melrose, Scottish Borders

Tel: (01896) 822624

Open: *Easter, and Whitsun to October*

Admission: *Charges*

Refreshments: *None*

Parking: *Small car park*

Disabled access: *Good, no special facilities*

An Ariel 550cc motorcycle of 1933 used by Jedburgh police until the early 1940s, now in the Melrose Motor Museum. (Above)

A Beardmore taxicab of 1951 which was used in Paisley, now in the Melrose Motor Museum. (Left).

The Motor Museum is just a short distance from Melrose's two famous landmarks – the Abbey and the rugby ground. It is run in conjunction with the **Myreton Motor Museum** and some of the vehicles move between the two. It is rather smaller than Myreton, with about 20 vehicles, but retains the same nostalgic atmosphere.

ROAD TRANSPORT COLLECTION

The collection of road vehicles does not represent a particular theme, but has been described as 'a miscellany of motoring'. One of the oldest cars on display is a 1909 Albion built in Glasgow. Another Scottish car is the 1923 Arrol-Johnston 'Allweather Tourer' built in Dumfries. In addition to several high performance cars, such as two Bentleys

from the 1920s and two Porches from the 1960s, there are several commercial vehicles. A Chrysler van from 1926 was used to deliver the Edinburgh *Evening News* for many years, and there is a very fine Morris bus from 1928. Two vehicles vie for the title of most unusual – a rickshaw from Sri Lanka and a French Citroën *Kegresse* of 1935. The *Kegresse* is a half-track (rear wheels replaced by tracks), designed for use in the Sahara Desert by the French Foreign Legion. Its ability to traverse rough terrain made it ideal for use on the Scottish grouse moors and it was never licensed for road use.

In addition to a good collection of motor cycles and several cycles there are many other motoring-related objects, from Corgi model cars to pedal cars, and even portable gramophones to take on a picnic.

MILL OF TOWIE

Auchindachy, near Keith, Aberdeenshire
Tel: (01542) 881307

Open: *Easter to Christmas, daily*

Admission: *Charges*

Refreshments: *Restaurant/Tea room*

Parking: *For cars and coaches*

Disabled access: *Limited*

Mill of Towie is a very good example of a large, fully-developed oatmeal mill, rebuilt at the turn of the century. It has a mid-breast wood and iron paddle water wheel, which drove the millstones commercially until the early 1970s. After a period of disuse the mill has been rehabilitated and is now open to the public.

The 'Mill on the Fleet', Gatehouse of Fleet, showing the waterwheel brought here from Milldriggan Mill.

MILL ON THE FLEET, GATEHOUSE OF FLEET

Gatehouse of Fleet, Dumfries & Galloway
Tel: (01557) 814009

Open: *March to October daily; November to December weekends only*

Admission: *Charges*

Refreshments: *Tea room*

Parking: *Car and coach park*

Disabled access: *Good*

Gatehouse derives its name from its position as estate village on the Cally estate, but owes its growth from the 1780s to a variety of industries, most notably cotton spinning. The larger of the two mill complexes was constructed by Birtwhistle & Sons in about 1785, with water power from a long lade constructed for the purpose. In common with most country cotton mills it could not compete with the larger steam-powered urban mills, and the Birtwhistle mill was converted to a bobbin mill in the later 19th century, continuing to serve the textile industries, but in a different way. Bobbin making in its turn declined, and the buildings decayed. By the mid 1960s the lower mill was so completely overgrown with ivy that it could hardly be seen. In the early 1980s, Stewartry District Council initiated a plan to consolidate the ruins and convert the lower mill to a tourist attraction. Initially 'job creation' labour was used, but when the Community Programme ended other means of completion had to be adopted. The 'Mill on the Fleet' is now a visitor centre with shop, restaurant and interpretation. An external stair tower has been added, and a waterwheel brought from Milldriggan Mill, Kirkinner, to replace the vanished original. The wheel is much too small, but does serve to indicate how the mill worked. A second wheel has been installed in the wheelpit of the upper mill.

MILL TRAIL VISITOR CENTRE

Glentana Mill, West Stirling Street,
Alva, Clackmannanshire
Tel: (01259) 769696

Open: *Daily*

Admission: *Free*

Refreshments: *Coffee Shop*

Parking: *Car and Coach park*

Disabled access: *Full disabled access*

Situated in parts of the single-storey red and white brick Glentana woollen mill, this visitor centre has replaced the converted Clock Mill in Tillicoultry as an interpretative centre for the Clackmannanshire textile trades. Part of the Mill still produces woollen garments, and the rest now houses a tourist information office, gift and coffee shops and the 'Mill Story'. This consists of an audio visual theatre and three of the looms from the former Clock Mill collection, with interpretative panels mounted on the walls.

MILTON OF CAMPSIE, STEAM PUMP

Milton of Campsie, Stirling

View from road

Preserved as a piece of sculpture outside a former carton factory, this two-cylinder non-rotary pump is one of a family widely used in industry, and still being made in small numbers. The factory in which it was used was originally a cotton printing works, but was adapted to make paper-pulp cartons, mainly for the drinks trade. The site is now an industrial estate.

Glentana Mill, Alva, home of the Mill Trail Visitor Centre. The woollen mills of the area were originally either water-powered, or housed hand-looms. By the time Glentana was built in the later 19th century steam power had taken over, and a steam engine was in use here until the 1970s. It is now in the collection of the National Museums of Scotland.

MONTGARRIE MILLS, NEAR ALFORD

Near Alford, Aberdeenshire
Tel: (019755) 62209

Open: Contact *Alan MacDonald & Son, tours by appointment, Monday to Friday and Saturday morning*

Admission: *Free*

Refreshments: *None*

Parking: *Car park*

Disabled access: *Limited*

The Aberdeenshire oatmeal-milling industry remained important until after the Second World War, largely because part of the wages of farm servants in the area was paid in meal. The number of operating mills has dwindled, and Montgarrie is now one of a handful still workable, and the only one working commercially. It is a late (*c.*1886) and large example, with a very large internal waterwheel (more than 7 m in diameter) which drove five pairs of stones, an unusually large number. Visitors are welcome, and may view the process as well as purchase the product.

Montgarrie Mills, showing the tall Aberdeenshire style of kiln ventilator.

MONTROSE AIR STATION MUSEUM

Waldron Road, Broomfield, Montrose, Angus
Tel: (01674) 672035

Open: *Sundays, or by appointment*

Admission: *Charges*

Refreshments: *Light refreshments*

Parking: *Car park*

Disabled access: *Not suitable at present*

In 1912 the Government planned twelve 'Air Stations' operated by the Royal Flying Corps and the first of these was at Montrose, which became operational in 1913. Because of its historical importance the entire aerodrome is now 'listed'. The Montrose Aerodrome Museum Society was formed in 1983 to preserve the history of aviation in the Montrose area. A Trust was set up and in 1992 the former RFC Watch Office and surrounding land was purchased to house the museum. Major exhibits are a Commer Karrier Airfield Control Van and a Westland *Wessex* helicopter. The collection of historic photographs and archive material is constantly being expanded.

MONTROSE MUSEUM

Panmure Place, Montrose, Angus
Tel: (01674) 673232
Fax: (01307) 464834

Open: *Monday to Saturday*

Admission: *Free*

Refreshments: *None*

Parking: *Outside and short stay car park nearby*

Disabled access: *Access to ground floor only, toilet*

Montrose Museum was opened in 1842 and, as with many of the museums in Scottish towns, its foundation was due to the local Natural History and Antiquarian Society. Extensive local collections cover the history of Montrose from prehistoric times to local government re-organisation. The gallery on the first floor is devoted to the maritime history of Montrose and the associated trades and industries. Like so many of the Scottish east coast ports, Montrose was an important base for whaling and some early whaling material is also displayed. Fishing, shipbuilding and foreign trade are represented with tools, illustrations and models – including a fine model of the *Cutty Sark* and a ship model made by French prisoners of war. On the upper floor are natural history dioramas and a changing exhibition gallery.

MORAY MOTOR MUSEUM

Bridge Street, Elgin, Moray
Tel: (01343) 544933
Fax: (01343) 546315

Open: *Easter to October, daily*

Admission: *Charges*

Refreshments: *Tea and coffee*

Parking: *Car park nearby*

Disabled access: *Access and facilities good*

Elgin boasts one of the oldest museums in Scotland and one of the newest. When the Elgin Museum collections were established in 1836, transport was not considered as worthy of museum status. The Moray Motor Museum collections of almost 150 years later demonstrate how attitudes have changed. The museum is situated a short distance to the north of the town centre, by the River Lossie. It is housed in an old mill building which has been attractively converted yet retains some of the original features such as the cast-iron columns supporting the roof.

The museum is a non-profit-making private venture resulting from the cars and motor cycles loaned by local enthusiasts. Most are beautifully restored and kept in working order.

ROAD TRANSPORT COLLECTION

There are about 20 cars on display and they cover a period of time from a 1904 Speedwell to a 1977 Triumph *Stag*. They also range from the relatively modest to some of the much-sought-after classic cars. If one looked for a theme, it could be

A Vincent HRD - a 'Rolls-Royce' of motorcycles - with several classic cars, including a Rolls-Royce, at the Moray Motor Museum.

open-topped cars for, despite the popular view of the inclement Scottish weather, drop-heads seem to dominate. Larger examples such as the 1928 4½ Litre Bentley and Rolls-Royce *Phantom 1* of 1927 stand out, but the sleek Jaguar SS100 of 1939, supported by some of its stable-mates, makes an impressive display.

The collection of some 20 motor cycles includes many of the most popular models from the 1913 Douglas with its twin cylinder engine and exposed flywheel, to the powerful V-twin Vincent HRD.

MUSEUM OF FIRE

Lothian and Borders Fire Brigade Headquarters, Lauriston Place, City of Edinburgh

Tel: (0131) 228 2401

Fax: (0131) 229 1514

Open: *Mondays to Fridays. Organised parties can arrange visits outside stated times (confirmation advised)*

Admission: *Free (at present)*

Refreshments: *Available locally*

Parking: *Public car parks nearby*

Disabled access: *Good. Facilities available*

A Merryweather 'Gem' horse-drawn steam pump dating from 1901 being demonstrated at the Museum of Fire.

The City of Edinburgh was the first municipal authority in the United Kingdom to establish a Fire Brigade. The year was 1824 in October, and later the same year, on November 15, Edinburgh suffered a great fire which burned for four days. Firemaster James Braidwood, founder of the new fire service, and his Brigade learned many lessons from their 'baptism of fire' and became a much admired and copied unit. Over the years, members of the Brigade collected items of interest and in 1965 Firemaster Rushbrook opened the Braidwood Museum at Edinburgh's McDonald Road fire station. In 1989 the museum was re-located at the Brigade's Lauriston Place headquarters, originally opened in 1900 as a fire station and homes for firefighters. The museum now occupies the operational areas of the fire station, made available by the building of a new fire station at Tollcross. When Lauriston was built, it was designed to house horse-drawn steam-powered fire pumps – a replica of the original stables has been reconstructed to show visitors how the horses were looked after. The museum plays an important role in the field of education, as an integral part of an innovative fire safety programme for school children. To bring the dangers of a fire to life, the museum has very effectively re-created a small street scene during the great fire of 1824. Although fighting fires does not come into the scope of 'transport', getting personnel

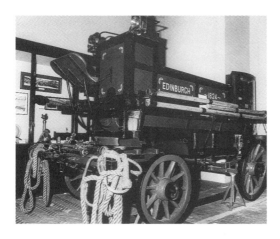

The first horse-drawn manual water pump purchased by the Edinburgh Fire Establishment in 1824, and now in the Museum of Fire.

MUSEUM OF FLIGHT (National Museums of Scotland)

East Fortune Airfield, North Berwick, East Lothian

Tel: (01620) 880308

Fax: (01620) 880355

NMS: (0131) 225 7534

Fax: (0131) 226 5949

Open: *April to September*
(*otherwise by prior appointment*)

Admission: *Charges*

Refreshments: *Tea room*

Parking: *Car park*

Disabled access: *Access and facilities very good*

and equipment to the fire certainly does. To emphasise this point, the Museum of Fire was the overall winner of the prestigious Scania Transport Trust Awards for 1991.

ROAD TRANSPORT

Although some of the smaller items on display go back to 1426, the oldest manual pump dates from 1806; another is the first manual pump, dated 1824, purchased by the newly formed Edinburgh Fire Establishment. There are also two horse-drawn steam pumps, an 1897 Shand Mason, and a 1901 Merryweather Gem which is on display and is contemporary with the building. The oldest fire-engine with an internal-combustion engine is a 1910 Halley made in Glasgow for the Leith Fire Brigade. A 1929 Dennis, a 1936 Dennis and a 1936 Leyland represent the classic fire engines ('pumps' or 'appliances' to fire-fighters), with their open bodies and ladders above. The 1939 Dennis still has a ladder on top, but looks more like a bus and is known as the 'Limousine'. Wartime and post-war appliances are also represented. Several of the vehicles are kept in working order and are a popular attraction at fêtes, displays and parades.

The aviation industry in Scotland may not have been as important as the traditional heavy industries, but companies such as Beardmore, G. & J. Weir, Blackburn, Scottish Aviation, Rolls-Royce and Ferranti did make a significant contribution. Scotland was well to the fore in the early use of air travel, which linked the Highlands and Islands with Edinburgh and Glasgow, thus playing an important part in the development of remote regions. Yet, even in the late 1960s Scotland did not have an aviation museum, or even an aviation display of any size in a comprehensive museum. The **Museum of Transport** in Glasgow had an autogiro and the Royal Scottish Museum (now the **Royal Museum of Scotland**) opened an aircraft gallery in 1966. This featured a good collection of aero engines, models and an early hang glider built by Percy Pilcher in 1896. Pilcher was an English marine engineer who worked as a lecturer at the University of Glasgow, and as a hobby built a series of successful gliders. His early flights, in 1895, were made on the gentle slopes of the northern banks of the River Clyde. Later he moved to England and died after a crash in his most successful glider, the *Hawk*, in 1899. The *Hawk* is the only one of Pilcher's gliders to survive.

In 1971 the Royal Scottish Museum acquired a Supermarine *Spitfire* and this led to a sequence of events culminating in the opening of a Museum of Flight at East Fortune Airfield in 1975. At the same time, another aircraft museum was being founded at Strathallan in Perthshire. The privately owned Strathallan Collection aimed to fly its aircraft, whereas the Museum of Flight adopted a more conventional museum approach concentrating on the history of flight with particular relevance to Scotland. Unfortunately, the Strathallan Collection was short-lived and most of the aircraft were sold in the 1980s.

The Museum of Flight's main display hangar featuring a Supermarine Spitfire in the foreground

MUSEUM SITE

The Museum of Flight is situated 23 miles (37 km) east of Edinburgh near the town of Haddington, on East Fortune Airfield. This is a very appropriate site as the hangars and other buildings were part of a large World War II airfield. It was also the site of a World War I Royal Naval Air Service station from which aeroplanes and airships operated. Towards the end of the war, three large airship sheds were built and in 1919 the rigid airship R34 arrived from Beardmore's works at Inchinnan, near Glasgow, where it had been constructed. On 2 July 1919 the R34 left East Fortune and headed west to become the first aircraft to cross the Atlantic from Europe to America. Alcock and Brown had made their non-stop flight in the opposite direction just over two weeks earlier in a converted Vickers *Vimy* bomber. The R34 added to its place in history by making the first double crossing of the Atlantic. Unfortunately, neither the R34 nor the airship sheds at East Fortune survived the 1920s. Several small R34 relics survive and are displayed along with other airship material.

From its early days, with only a handful of aeroplanes, the Museum of Flight has grown steadily over the years to include about 40 aeroplanes, an extensive collection of aero engines, airship material and rockets. Although the main runway does not belong to the museum, it has been available for several aircraft to arrive by air, including two very impressive landings by the de Havilland *Comet* airliner and the Avro *Vulcan* bomber. The buildings on the site, including the control tower (disused), four hangars and several smaller buildings have recently been given 'listed building' status. The museum originally owned one hangar, then two, and now all four. Improvements have been made to the buildings and facilities, resulting in the reopening of the two original hangars in 1993, after repairs. Following the acquisition of the other two hangars, a rolling development programme is under way.

The excellent new displays include an Air Traffic Control Centre situated on a mezzanine floor, which also makes a very good viewing point. Other features include: a Royal Observer Corps post; a tribute to Sheila Scott OBE, the record-breaking pilot who died in 1988, and several displays describing various aspects of the work of the RAF, including the Central Flying School. The museum has a collection of thousands of model aircraft, of which almost 1,000 are on display; these range from plastic kits to wind-tunnel test models.

Although most of the aircraft are behind minimal barriers, there are a number of exhibits which visitors are encouraged to handle.

AEROPLANE AND AERO ENGINE COLLECTION

The early years in the history of flight are represented by Pilcher's *Hawk* glider of 1896, models and aero engines. There are seven aero engines built before 1914 including a four-cylinder Wright engine of 1910 presented to the Royal Scottish Museum by Orville Wright.

The earliest aeroplane in the collection is a de Havilland *Puss Moth* of 1930, a type used for many record-breaking flights and private flying. Scottish-built aircraft from the 1930s are extremely rare and the museum has an interesting example, the Weir W-2 autogiro built by G. & J. Weir of Cathcart in 1934.

The Avro Vulcan delta-winged jet bomber was flown into East Fortune Airfield at the end of its service life in 1984. (Above left)

An English Electric Lightning supersonic jet fighter on display in the 'Jets and Aerospace' hangar. (Above right))

Weirs went on to build experimental helicopters, but none survive.

The Supermarine *Spitfire* and the Messerschmitt Me 163 *Komet* rocket-powered fighter attract the most interest from the World War II aircraft. From the post-war jet age the Avro *Vulcan*, which took part in the Falklands conflict, is the most impressive sight, followed by the de Havilland *Comet IV* and the English Electric *Lightning* jet fighter. A recent addition to the jet fighter collection is a Czech-built Russian MiG.15, together with the cockpit of a two-seater version, an engine and a flying suit. One of the few Scottish-designed and built aircraft to serve world-wide was the Scottish Aviation *Twin Pioneer*. A 1959 example of this twin piston-engined airliner, designed to operate from short runways, is on display. At certain times some of the aircraft are opened up for visitors to obtain a closer look.

The strength of the collection lies in the variety of its aircraft with examples of private aircraft, large and small airliners, fighters, bombers, trainers, autogiros, helicopters, hang gliders, sailplanes and (in reserve) a man-powered aircraft. The aero engine collection also covers most of the variations in design from a three-cylinder Anzani of 1910 to one of the Rolls-Royce *Olympus* jet engines from the prototype *Concorde*.

The work of restoring the aircraft and engines is carried out not only by museum staff but also by volunteer members of the Aircraft Preservation Society of Scotland. The volunteers played a major role in the early years of the Museum of Flight when there were no full-time staff on site. More recently,

they have collected and restored several aircraft of their own, including an Auster AOP5 and a Miles *Monarch*, which are now on display. Work is also being carried out on the museum's aircraft, engines, models and records.

ROCKETS AND SATELLITES

From the outset 'Flight' included spaceflight and rocket-powered missiles (it also included unwanted exponents of the art of flying – starlings and sparrows in particular!). Three British rockets were acquired in the 1970s: *Black Knight* of 1958, *Black Arrow* (incomplete) of *c*.1964 and *Blue Streak* of 1964. The impressive *Blue Streak* was designed as a ballistic missile, but later adapted as the first stage of a three-stage European satellite launcher *Europa*. Unfortunately, the other stages were not as reliable as the British first stage and the *Europa* project was cancelled. There are also several models, rocket motors and experimental satellites.

Missiles include the English Electric *Thunderbird* ground-to-air missile and the *Blue Steel* air-to-ground 'stand-off bomb'. The latter was designed to be carried by the V-bombers, such as the *Vulcan*.

Painting of the stillhouse at Ardbeg Distillery, in the Museum of Islay Life.

MUSEUM OF ISLAY LIFE

Port Charlotte, Isle of Islay, Argyll & Bute
Tel: (01496) 850358

Open: *Easter to October, daily; November to March, Monday to Wednesday*

Admission: *Charges*

Refreshments: *None*

Parking: *Car park*

Disabled access: *Good*

One of the best voluntary museums in Scotland, this is in a former church on the outskirts of Port Charlotte. Its principal displays are on domestic life and agriculture, but the locally-important whisky-distilling industry also features. Exhibits include an illicit still, a variety of advertising-jugs and containers, and most notably a painting of the stillhouse of Ardbeg Distillery, one of only a handful of paintings depicting the interiors of distilleries. There are also craft tools for wheelwrights, coopers and leather workers.

MUSEUM OF LEAD MINING, WANLOCKHEAD

Wanlockhead, Dumfries & Galloway
Tel: (0165) 974 387

Open: *End March to November, daily*

Admission: *Charges, but not for exterior viewing*

Refreshments: *Restaurant*

Parking: *At museum, for cars and coaches*

Disabled access: *Good in museum and cottages. Restricted elsewhere*

Leadhills and Wanlockhead, two of the highest villages in Scotland, owe their existence to a remarkable area of mineralisation on the borders of the old counties of Lanarkshire and Dumfriesshire. 'God's Treasure House in Scotland' produced gold, some of which is in the Scottish Regalia, silver, and most importantly, lead. Lead was mined in this area from the Middle Ages, and in the 18th and 19th centuries the most powerful technology of the period was harnessed to win, with increasing difficulty, the ore of the area. The landscape on both sides of the county boundary is littered with fragments of mining activity. Many of these have been so well demolished – often by army teams practising sabotage – that they are difficult but not impossible to analyse. Others have been covered by

The 'Bobbing John' mine pumping engine at the Straitsteps lead mine, Wanlockhead, now in the care of Historic Scotland.

later waste heaps, which have protected them, but are at risk from modern land reclamation schemes. Below ground lie miles of tunnels and caverns following the mineral veins. Many of these are flooded, but some can be explored. A few contain machinery. The villages themselves are part of the mining story. Both contain small, individually built cottages, and Wanlockhead has a few 'miners' rows'. Both have miners' libraries, co-operative ventures to provide books for leisure use, for lead miners worked a short day in comparison to other industrial workers. Leadhills has its warning bell, to give news of underground disaster. And Wanlockhead has the Museum of Lead Mining.

The Museum of Lead Mining is unusual in that it combines a central display with a number of outstations to tell the tale of mining in all its ramifications. The core displays illustrate the techniques of mining and the life of the miner, with working models of mine pumps to illustrate surviving plant no longer operable. A short distance away, down an old railway track, is an accessible lead mine, into which guided tours are taken. Further down the track are the consolidated remains of the Pates Knowes Lead Smelter, and of the 'Bobbing John' beam engine at Straitsteps. The smelter is, like the museum, the property of the Scottish Museum of Lead Mining, but the 'Bobbing John' engine is in the care of the Secretary of State for Scotland, and is looked after by Historic Scotland. Close to the engine is a block of three miners' cottages laid out

by the museum to show the changes in housing from the early 18th century. Visitors can also see the site of the Bay Mine, where one of William Symington's early steam engines was installed, and where a large water-wheel pit provides an indication of the significance of water power in early lead mining.

MUSEUM OF TRANSPORT, GLASGOW

Kelvin Hall, 1 Bunhouse Road, City of Glasgow
Tel: (0141) 287 2720
Fax: (0141) 287 2692

Open: *Daily*

Admission: *Free*

Refreshments: *Restaurant*

Parking: *Car park*

Disabled access: *Access and facilities good*

The City of Glasgow founded a museum in the 1870s and in 1902 a purpose-built Art Gallery and Museum was opened at Kelvingrove in Glasgow's West End. The transport collections, with a strong maritime bias, were included in this building. As the collections grew, more space was needed, consequently, a separate Museum of Transport was opened in 1964, appropriately housed in the former Glasgow Corporation Tramway Works at Coplawhill on the south side of the city. Despite its remoteness from the city centre, the museum attracted a rapidly growing number of visitors which clearly justified its existence. By the 1980s the building reached its centenary and also the end of its useful life – extensive repairs were needed and it was too small. A new Exhibition Centre was built in Glasgow and this replaced the Kelvin Hall. Situated across the road from the Art Gallery and Museum, the vast expanse of the Kelvin Hall was then converted into a sports centre and the new Museum of Transport. The movement of all the locomotives, buses, trams and delicate ship models was a major undertaking which was completed in time for the opening in 1988.

Naturally, the collections have a very strong bias towards items built or used in Glasgow and the surrounding area, but with some collections a wider Scottish or even British outlook has been adopted. Foreign cars can be justified if they were used on the streets of Glasgow. Many of the exhibits have been expertly restored by the technical staff of the museum.

When planning the new museum, a conscious effort was made to improve on the old displays at Coplawhill by creating sympathetic environments for certain exhibits. One such display greets visitors as they enter the museum, where they can wander down *Kelvin Street* on Friday afternoon the 9th of December 1938. In addition to vehicles parked in the street, this presentation makes use of other museum collections in the shop windows; for example, hand tools, electrical appliances and costumes. Also in the fictitious street is the entrance to a recreated station on Glasgow's Subway (as the underground railway was called). Most of the spacious ground floor is devoted to land transport, while on a mezzanine floor there are displays of cycles, motorcycles and prams. Also on the mezzanine floor is the Clyde Room housing the ship models. Adjacent to the restaurant is an exhibition of 'Food on the Move' illustrating eating while travelling – from a railway buffet to Concorde.

A unique car designed for hill-climb races by William Anderson of Newton Mearns in the 1930s, and now in the Museum of Transport, Glasgow.

ROAD TRANSPORT

Although the two horse-drawn Romany caravans look old-fashioned they are, in fact, relatively modern having been built in the 20th century, whereas most of the other coaches and carriages date from the mid 19th century. Probably the most impressive is the Glasgow and London Royal Mail coach of 1840.

The collection of cycles is one of the largest in the country and the display has recently been made more attractive by grouping a selection of the machines thematically, and introducing interactive features. One of the bicycles on display is claimed to be the oldest surviving bicycle in the world. The first pedal-operated bicycle was invented and built by Kirkpatrick Macmillan in about 1840. Macmillan was a blacksmith from Courthill in Dumfriesshire who covered many miles on his bicycle but, unfortunately, it did not survive. The example in the museum is one of several copies built during the years following Macmillan's invention. The motorcycle collection is good but not remarkable as, of course, Scottish-built motorcycles are almost non-existent.

By contrast, in the early years of this century, Scotland was a leading motor car manufacturing country with three important companies: Albion, Argyll and Arrol-Johnston, followed in the 1920s by Beardmore. The museum's unique collection of almost a score of Scottish-built cars are displayed together. Examples of other makes of car range from a Ford *Model T* to a Rolls-Royce *Phantom II*. Many of these are displayed in an impressive showroom setting, complete with their price (when new!).

When it was decided to replace Glasgow's tramcars by motor buses in 1958, the museum was able to make plans to preserve a limited selection and it was this exercise which stimulated the founding of the 1964 Museum of Transport. Seven trams are now on display, the earliest being a horse-drawn tram of 1895 and the latest a double-decker *Cunarder* built as late as 1952 at the Coplawhill Works – to which it returned as a museum specimen. Two double-decker motor buses are displayed: a Scottish-built Albion of 1949, and the first Leyland *Atlantean* of 1958. There is a third double-decker bus, but closer inspection of the roof reveals that it is an electric trolleybus.

Of the commercial vehicles, probably the most impressive is the 1920 Ruston and Hornsby traction engine together with its threshing machine, baler and travelling hut. Another steam-powered vehicle of interest is a 1916 steam lorry made by Sentinel – a local firm which later moved to Shropshire. There are several vans and lorries and an impressive collection of fire engines.

General view of tram and locomotive displays in the Museum of Transport, Glasgow.

RAILWAYS

Six Scottish locomotives and a royal coach are the principal exhibits, supported by some fine models. Of the steam locomotives the one which attracts most attention is *No. 123* of the Caledonian Railway Company. Not only was this attractive engine built in Glasgow, but also it took part in the famous 1888 London to Edinburgh races between the rival east and west coast routes. The passenger locomotives are all painted in the liveries of Scottish railway companies prior to the amalgamations of 1923.

Glasgow's underground railway, the 'Subway', was opened in 1896 and the museum has recreated one of the original stations, Merkland Street. A coach from 1898, when the system was cable operated, is displayed, together with an early electric coach and a relatively modern one from the 1950s.

SHIPPING

The very large collection of ship models is a mixed blessing, for row upon row of ship models can be too much for the average visitor. A good attempt has been made in the Clyde Room to group the models into attractive presentations; for example, the *Queen Mary, Queen Elizabeth* and *Queen Elizabeth 2* are displayed side by side in one case. Incidentally, the model of the *QE2* is an example of

A display of paddle steamers in the Clyde Room in the Museum of Transport.

the craftsmanship of the museum's technical staff. Most of the large models were built at considerable expense by the shipbuilders who later donated them to the museum, but the only available model of the *QE2* was a basic hull used for test purposes in a long water tank. The staff converted this into a fully detailed model – complete with deck chairs – and also built the model of the royal yacht *Britannia*.

As the name of the gallery implies, most of the models were built or used, or both, on the River Clyde. The number of famous ships built on the Clyde is something of an eye opener when one surveys the shipbuilding scene today. Some of the favourite models for local visitors are the Clyde steamers which gave many of them a day out in the fresh air 'doon the watter'. A total of about 250 models are on display out of a collection of some 800 models, so an effort is made to change the displays from time to time.

AVIATION

Air transport does not receive a high priority: there is a model of Glasgow Airport, and the museum has two full-size aircraft. These are a Scottish-built autogiro built by David Kay in 1934 and a replica of Percy Pilcher's *Hawk* glider of 1896 (the original is at the **Museum of Flight**). Pilcher worked in Glasgow as a marine engineer and made his first flights on the banks of the River Clyde.

MYRETON MOTOR MUSEUM

Aberlady, East Lothian
Tel: (01875) 870288

Open: *Daily*

Admission: *Charges*

Refreshments: *None*

Parking: *Car park*

Disabled access: *To all displays except cycle gallery, toilet*

Myreton Motor Museum is situated about 18 miles (29 km) east of Edinburgh, just a few miles inland from the popular sandy beaches of East Lothian. Myreton and the **Melrose Motor Museum** are privately owned and have a distinctive character of which they are proud. Their guide book says 'The exhibits to be seen are not of the large, exotic or expensive type in the main', also 'There has been no attempt to restore the cars to showroom condition'. The cars look as though they have just been driven into the museum from the road, and indeed some have. Most of them are in working order and frequently appear at rallies, in parades or in films. Modern display techniques have not been needed to re-create a vintage atmosphere; the museum looks and smells like a vintage garage. The cars are not parked in neat rows with barriers keeping visitors at arms length. However, you are asked not to open the doors or lift the bonnets, but one of the staff will be pleased to do this for you if requested. The layout consists of a number of separate display areas, each with a different and variable display.

There are about 35 cars on display at Myreton. The oldest are an 1895 Léon Bollée motor tricycle which was once owned by the Hon. C. S. Rolls, and an 1897 Arnold-Benz car, both of which are on loan from the National Museums of Scotland. One of the more recent, and unusual, vehicles is the *Scamp,* an electric car built by Scottish Aviation in 1965. There are several Scottish-built vehicles on display, such as the 1909 Albion wagonette which started life as an open-topped hotel bus in Inverness-shire, but was later adapted as a farm tractor and finally restored to its original layout. The Dumfries-built Galloway

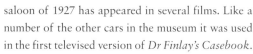

An Alvis 12/50 sports car of 1924 restored to running order and now in the Myreton Museum as are the other two cars illustrated. (Above left)

A rare Scottish car, the 1927 Galloway, seen here with Ian Carmichael during the filming of Dorothy L Sayers' "Five Red Herrings" for BBC Television. (Above)

A 1926 Morris Oxford during filming for James Cameron's memoirs and being driven by him in the Highlands. (Left)

saloon of 1927 has appeared in several films. Like a number of the other cars in the museum it was used in the first televised version of *Dr Finlay's Casebook*.

In addition to the private cars there is a mixture of other road vehicles; a Ford Model T van of 1924, an Austin lorry of 1928 and an early Morris Commercial Type SW Series built in 1925 as an army lorry, but converted into a genuine shooting brake and used until 1969 on a Scottish sporting estate. There are one or two sports and racing cars on display such as the sleek Alvis 12/50 sports car of 1924 and the even smaller 500cc Norton-engined Cooper racing car of 1954.

Motor cycles dominate one of the display areas and the collection of about 30 machines includes several from the years before World War I. The cycle collection contains most of the main variations in cycle design from 1866 to 1950. There is also an assortment of transport related 'odds and ends': a pram, an invalid chair, four outboard motors, one or two aero engines, petrol pumps and an RAC Box from the notorious Soutra Hill. Smaller items are to be found in every nook and cranny: petrol cans, tools, instruction manuals, leaflets, posters and old metal road-side signs from the 1920s and 30s.

Finally, there is a very good collection of World War II military vehicles and again 'not of the large, exotic or expensive type'. In other words, not the tanks and mobile cranes, but the smaller armoured scout cars and run-of-the-mill vehicles often neglected by museums. The 1939 Morris ambulance was a standard 10 cwt commercial chassis converted to an ambulance. This vehicle, together with the 12 hp Standard utility used by the RAF and the 10 hp Austin truck have all appeared in parades including several in France. There are also several military motor cycles.

NEW ABBEY CORN MILL

New Abbey, Dumfries & Galloway

Tel: (0131) 244 3101

Open: *All year, April to September daily; October to March, closed Thursday p.m. and Friday*

Admission: *Charges*

Refreshments: *None*

Parking: *Limited, at mill, large car park about 250 metres away*

Disabled access: *Very limited*

This was the village mill for a small Galloway community. It is not at all typical of such mills, as it incorporates the miller's house at one end of the building, and has a pitch-back wheel (itself unusual) on the side rather than on a gable, or internally mounted. After years of neglect, the local landowner, Charles Stewart, began a programme of restoration in the mid 1960s. He subsequently gave the mill to the nation, and restoration was completed in the early 1980s. Because of the severing of the original watercourse it has proved necessary to install an electric pump to supply water to the

New Abbey Corn Mill, New Abbey, Kirkcudbrightshire, probably on the site of a medieval monastic mill.

mill pond. The machinery is unusual, with two pairs of stones fitted with lever rather than screw adjustment. The original woodwork has been retained, hence modern hygiene regulations prevent meal being ground for human consumption.

NEW LANARK

Near Lanark, South Lanarkshire

Tel: (01555) 661345

Open: *All year, daily. Visitor centre daily except Christmas and New Year*

Admission: *Charges for individual attractions, exterior viewing free*

Refreshments: *Tea room*

Parking: *Car and coach park above village with footpath to link. Disabled visitors may park in village*

Disabled access: *Good access to most public areas*

New Lanark does not consider itself a museum, a view that is endorsed by the Scottish Museums Council, as it has no professional curatorial staff. It is, however, clearly a site of enormous importance, containing objects of great interest, both intrinsically and by association.

took up Arkwright's ideas, finding men willing to invest in the new process, and himself building the New Lanark mills on the most tractable of the falls of Clyde. Arkwright's patents were quashed in 1785, freeing Dale to develop the site unrestricted.

Dale's work at New Lanark is of exceptional interest. He introduced a level of refinement in the design of both mills and housing which Arkwright had not envisaged. Though there is no documentary evidence, the parallels to the design of the Inveraray tenements and the Fort George barrack blocks in the construction of the New Lanark housing suggests that Dale consulted Robert Adam, then active in designing Glasgow buildings, about the best approach, for Adam's family had been involved both with Inveraray and with Fort George. The central planning of the first mills is another feature linking to Scottish Palladianism, representing a departure from Arkwright's practice at Cromford and elsewhere. One could, indeed, argue that it was Dale who introduced into factory design the concepts of dignity and monumentality which persisted, especially in Scotland, for well over a century, and which were certainly inherited by Owen, whose school and Institute for the Formation of Character have that same central planning, and whose other major buildings in the village – the mechanic's workshop and the No. 3 Mill adopt a similar exterior form.

It is a tribute to the excellence of Dale's vision that the complex survived for about 180 years with only relatively minor alterations. In 1963 the New Lanark Association was founded with the objective of modernising the interiors of the house, but in 1968 the Gourock Ropework Company decided to close the mills. The decline of the village thereafter was apparently irreversible, but a Scottish Civic Trust initiative in 1974 led first to a plan to revive and develop the work of the New Lanark Association, and then to the formation of the New Lanark Conservation and Civic Trust. The availability of grants for house improvement, and of funding from the Manpower Services Commission, enabled the work of reconditioning the housing to continue, and the approach of selling both unrestored and restored house shells to private owners proved effective. Over a period of several

The rear of numbers 3 and 2 mills at New Lanark, monuments to clarity and rationality in the thinking of its begetters.

The name of the village has been familiar to generations of Scottish schoolchildren through its link with Robert Owen, social reformer and idealist. Yet it was not Robert Owen, but his father-in-law David Dale, who created the village and provided not only a physical but a philosophical framework for Owen to develop. The origins of the physical concept, indeed, go back to the 1760s and 1770s when Richard Arkwright developed his 'water frame' for spinning cotton yarn, and the carding and drawing machinery to supply it with cotton fibres in a suitable form. Profiting by the experience of such as James Hargreaves, who reaped little reward for his invention of the spinning-jenny, Arkwright first built his own mills, then sought to sell his package of inventions to men of substance, who could be trusted, within reason, to operate his processes properly, and to pay their dues. In Scotland his first port of call was Glasgow, then the centre of the fine linen trade, and a centre for the importation of colonial produce, including cotton. The leading entrepreneur there was David Dale, and he eagerly years first the school and workshops, then the Dale and Owen houses, then the mills and institute came into public ownership, and the daunting task of rehabilitating the heart of the village began.

Now this is nearing completion. The school, whose roof collapsed in 1971, has been restored to good external condition through what is now Historic Buildings and Monuments. The shells of the other buildings have been consolidated, and new uses found for most. There are craft workshops in the dyeworks, and a visitor centre (including the Annie McLeod Experience, a dark ride), and offices in No. 3 Mill. Other buildings house a motor museum and a model railway. Environmental improvement has cleared rubbish during a period when the mill area was owned by Metal Extractions, who dumped scrap metal and process waste, and the wheelpit of No. 4 Mill has been excavated. Into it has been put a large water wheel from a flint mill near Kirkcaldy. Most recently, the restoration of No. 1 Mill, cut down in height in the mid 1940s, has been completed and a Youth Hostel has been created in Wee Row. The sum of all these efforts has been to get very close to the 'complete revivification' of the village decided on as the preferred option when its future was planned in 1975.

New Lanark, with the school (centre) Caithness Row (foreground) and mechanics' workshop beyond.

NEWTON STEWART, THE MUSEUM

York Road, Newton Stewart, Dumfries & Galloway,
Tel: None (Contact Mr. J. D. McLay (01671) 402472)

Open: *May and June, Monday to Saturday; July to September, every day*	
Admission: *Charges*	
Refreshments: *None*	
Parking: *Street parking*	
Disabled access: *Access to ground floor*	

Newton Stewart is situated on the River Cree, in a rich agricultural area. At one time there was a limited textile industry in the area but it has not survived. The town was also situated on the important road and rail routes for traffic to Northern Ireland via Stranraer; the railway has now gone and the trunk road bypasses the town centre.

The museum is housed in the former St John's Church and is run by a charitable trust made up of volunteers from the town with the aim of recording and displaying the history of the town and surrounding countryside. Local industries are covered, with photographs, tools and agricultural implements. Transport items on display include

early cycles and two motorcycles from the 1920s, an AJS and the much rarer Connaught of 1921. There are also displays of motoring accessories, saddlery and photographs of the former railway. A blacksmith's shop has been set up to represent a local 'smiddy' complete with many hand and larger tools. The museum also has a considerable collection of woodworking tools.

NORTH CARR LIGHTSHIP, DUNDEE

Victoria Dock, Dundee City
Office: Port of Dundee Ltd., Harbour Chambers,
Dock Street, Dundee

Information: *Please contact the office in writing for further details*

Lightships were often used in coastal waters to warn mariners of underwater hazards such as sandbanks or rocks. This vessel was built on the Clyde in 1937 and for 42 years was moored near the North Carr reef off Fife Ness to warn passing shipping of the dangerous rocks. Towering above the deck is the all-important light and a huge fog horn. Below deck are the crew's quarters, radio room, stores and engine room. This latter installation is somewhat misleading as the lightship was not self-propelled – it had to be towed to its allotted station. However, it required engines to generate electricity in order to power the large light and the other equipment needed to run the ship.

The introduction of modern automatic lighting during the 1970s made manned lighthouses and lightships redundant. The North Carr Lightship was Scotland's last lightship when she was taken out of service in 1975. Luckily, she was saved from the scrapyard by the efforts of North East Fife District Council and for many years she was moored in the harbour at Anstruther where visitors could inspect her. More recently the North Carr Lightship has been taken over by the Port of Dundee Ltd. and moved to Victoria Dock in Dundee. It is hoped to moor the lightship adjacent to the frigate *Unicorn* and open her as a visitor attraction in the near future.

The North Carr Lightship at Anstruther before its move to the Victoria Dock, Dundee.

OLD BLACKSMITH'S SHOP, COACH MUSEUM, GRETNA GREEN

Gretna Green, Dumfries & Galloway
Tel: (01461) 338441
Fax: (01461) 338442

Open: *All year*

Admission: *Charges*

Refreshments: *Restaurant and Coffee House*

Parking: *Car park*

Disabled access: *Access and facilities good*

Without a doubt, the romantic tales of runaways being married at the Gretna Green 'Smiddy' draw visitors to this centre. With about 400,000 visitors per year it is one of Scotland's most popular tourist attractions, yet few of these visitors realise that Gretna Green also has one of the few collections of coaches open to the public in Scotland. It is very appropriate, of course, because Gretna Green was an important stopping place in the days of stage-coaches. The 1830 Toll House also survives (this also has a marriage room) and nearby is Thomas Telford's fine bridge across the River Sark.

Pride of place in the coach collection goes to the public service stage-coach dating from *c.*1800 and used in the Lake District and Borders. The more ceremonial state landau was used by the Judges at Carlisle Assizes in the mid 19th century. There is a second landau, two broughams, a Victoria and a one-horse American buckboard. In addition to the actual coaches there are a number of models and miscellaneous items connected with horse-drawn vehicles.

OLD MILLS, ELGIN

Elgin, Moray
Tel: (01309) 673701

Open: *April to September, daily except Sundays*

Admission: *Charges*

Refreshments: *None*

Parking: *Good car park*

Disabled access: *Limited*

This picturesque building was rescued from decay and neglect by Moray District in the 1980s, reconditioned, and is now open to visitors. It has two wheels, one broad all-metal one, the other of an unusual type, most commonly found in north-east Scotland, the single-ring paddle wheel. The kiln, too, is typical of the Elgin area, with its pyramidal roof and louvred ventilator.

The picturesque Old Mills at Elgin, showing the small single-ring waterwheel, and the pyramidal kiln for drying oats before grinding oatmeal. (Above)

King William IV's coach, later used by the Judges at Carlisle Assizes and now on display at Gretna Green. (Left)

PAISLEY MUSEUM

High Street, Paisley, Renfrewshire

Tel: (0141) 889 3151

Open: *All year, daily except Sundays, public holidays*

Admission: *Free*

Refreshments: *None*

Parking: *Small car park*

Disabled access: *Limited*

Paisley Museum is an old-established local authority museum, endowed by the Coats family, the noted local threadmakers, and housed in a fine classical building. Apart from its art galleries, the museum has three principal spaces. Two of these contain some material of industrial interest. The galleried entrance hall has on its upper level displays on Renfrewshire history and archaeology, including the local thread, soap, cornflour, jam and shipbuilding industries. Of these, the thread industry was of world significance, and the others of British national importance. Apart from thread manufacture, Paisley's most renowned industry was the weaving of shawls. There is a whole gallery devoted to this, with related textiles. The display includes handlooms and associated equipment, as well as part of the museum's remarkable collection of shawls, illustrating the remarkable advances in the sophistication of Jacquard loom weaving during the early and mid 19th century. Several of the

Cases of exhibits illustrating local industries. The Robertsons' jams 'golly', still a trade mark, is prominent, though the firm is no longer in Paisley.

museum's collection of looms are not on public display, but may be seen by appointment.

PEOPLE'S PALACE, GLASGOW

Glasgow Green, City of Glasgow

Tel: (0141) 554 0223

Fax: (0141) 550 0892

Open: *All year, daily*

Admission: *Free*

Refreshments: *Restaurant in Winter Garden*

Parking: *Car park*

Disabled access: *Limited*

Glasgow Museums' main displays of material of industrial interest are in the Transport Museum, but the People's Palace on Glasgow Green has much of interest and relevance to the city's industries. Though primarily concerned with social history, there is an important new display on Glasgow's industries, with an accompanying audio-visual show. The museum has an unrivalled collection of Glasgow-made stained glass, including a fine series of panels illustrating trades characteristic of the Maryhill district in the north west of the city. Though not strictly relevant to the subject of this volume, the People's Palace contains much material on the social and economic context within which industries rose and declined, and on phenomena such as trades unionism, popular entertainment and spectator sport intimately linked with Glasgow's experience as an industrial city.

THE PEOPLE'S STORY, CANONGATE TOLBOOTH

163 Canongate, City of Edinburgh
Tel: (0131) 529 4057
Fax: (0131) 557 3346

Open: *Monday to Saturday*

Admission: *Free*

Refreshments: *Nearby*

Parking: *Public car parks nearby*

Disabled access: *Access and facilities good*

The City of Edinburgh Museums and Galleries incorporate a number of museums covering the local history of Edinburgh. The People's Story is housed in the Canongate Tolbooth which was built in 1591 and used for the general collection of public dues rather than just road tolls. It also served as the burgh courthouse and prison for 300 years. Nearby is White Horse Close, which includes some of the buildings of the White Horse Inn, dating from 1623, which was the main coaching inn for travellers to and from London.

The People's Story describes the lives, work and leisure of ordinary people living in Edinburgh from the 1780s to the 1980s. Many of them worked in industries such as brewing, printing, shipbuilding, and biscuit and confectionery manufacture. There are two very good re-created industrial scenes showing a cooper and a bookbinder at work.

A transport exhibit features a tram conductress in the First World War and includes many interesting photographs, artifacts and ephemera relating to Edinburgh Tramways.

The centrepiece of the new display on Glasgow's industries in the People's Palace, Glasgow. (Upper)

Tram conductress display in the People's Story, based on Mary Gillon who worked on Edinburgh's trams during the First World War. (Lower)

P

99

PERTH MUSEUM AND ART GALLERY

George Street, Perth, Perthshire & Kinross
Tel: (01738) 632488
Fax: (01738) 635225

Open: *All year, closed Sundays*

Admission: *Free*

Refreshments: *None*

Parking: *Public car park nearby*

Disabled access: *Access limited to ground floor; toilet*

This impressive domed building is the oldest purpose-built museum in Scotland, having been built in 1824 to house the Literary and Antiquarian Museum. The aim of the museum is to cover the history of the Perth and Kinross district. A very informative permanent local history gallery was opened a few years ago on the ground floor called 'The Time of Our Lives'. This aims to introduce the history of transport and communication together with the development of industry and trade within the district. Due to the limited space available there are no large objects but good use is made of small artifacts, photographs, graphics and ephemera.

The story of transport begins with a 7,000-year-old dugout canoe and ends with the impressive Friarton Bridge, built in 1978 to carry the motorway across the River Tay. Despite the fact that Perth is some 25 miles (40 km) from the sea, it was an important port with a harbour and shipbuilding industry. Objects on display include fragments of medieval boats and ship models.

Land travel displays range from Roman roads to multi-storey car parks. Perth grew up because it was the first place to cross the River Tay by bridge. The ferries and bridges are illustrated and supported by a number of items from the days of horse-drawn transport, including a coaching inn sign. There is also a small display on Jas. McIntosh of Crieff, carriage maker, including his tools. The first steam railway in the district, the Dundee–Newtyle line, was built in 1831: the rise and fall of the railway system is shown with graphics, station signs and locomotive models. The air travel display covers the

early attempts to fly in the area, including David Kay's autogiros of the 1930s, and the development of Perth Aerodrome. (Kay's gyroplane of 1935 is preserved at the **Museum of Transport**, Glasgow.)

'Industry and Trade' starts with flint nodules of 700BC and continues with archaeological finds which are used very successfully to interpret the development of industry and technology through to the modern era. Water-related industries described include salmon and pearl fishing, brewing, distilling and blending. Objects range from Customs and Excise equipment to an illicit still. Perth was an important centre for the textile industry; this is illustrated with a spinning wheel and models of a Jacquard loom, a beetling machine and a mill steam engine. Several factories are featured including the well-known Pullars of Perth, Cleaners and Dyers. There is also a section on the local Moncrieff's Glassworks with equipment and products.

The museum has a number of objects in store which may be seen by appointment, including cycles and tramway rails.

PETER ANDERSON OF SCOTLAND CASHMERE WOOLLEN MILL AND MUSEUM

Nether Mill, Huddersfield St, Galashiels, Scottish Borders
Tel: (01896) 822091

Open: *June to September, daily; October to May daily, except Sunday*

Admission: *Charges*

Refreshments: *None*

Parking: *Car park*

Disabled access: *None*

The Borders woollen industry is world-renowned for the quality of its products, both knitted and woven. Most of the traditional Borders mills are no longer in production, but Nether Mill, Galashiels is. Visitors may view the processes in the mill, and see a museum display that incorporates a restored Leffel water turbine, the only direct-drive turbine displayed *in situ* in Scotland. It also includes a working 'traditional' power loom. The mill itself dates in part from 1805, with an addition dated 1866, and a good range of weaving sheds.

THE PIER HOUSE, SYMBISTER, SHETLAND

Symbister, Whalsay, Shetland
Tel: c/o J. A. Anderson (Secretary)
(01595) 693535 Ext. 317
Fax: c/o J. A. Anderson
(01595) 696472

Open: *Weekdays and Sundays (p.m.)*

Admission: *Charges*

Refreshments: *None*

Parking: *Car park*

Disabled access: *Limited; no toilet*

Whalsay is one of the islands on the eastern side of Shetland. The Pier House has been restored by the Hanseatic Booth Restoration and Conservation Trust set up in 1982. Their aim is to record the trade links between Shetland and Germany during the Hanseatic period from the 13th to 18th centuries. The Hansa (Association) was a highly organised trading league whose members sailed to some 200 towns, mainly in northern Europe. Their bases were known as *booths* – from the old Norse word *böd* meaning booth, hut or storehouse (the German word was *bude*). The Pier House is situated at the end of the pier, with sea on three sides, and was probably built by Hamburg merchants in the 17th century. However, there was a booth on Whalsay many years earlier.

Inside the Pier House there is an exhibition with display panels telling the story of the Hanseatic League, backed up by a reconstruction of a period setting with figures in costume and examples of the goods which were traded. There is also a display giving information on the island of Whalsay.

Nether Mill, Galashiels, home of the Peter Anderson woollen mill and museum.

The small steam hammer from the workshops at the Gourock Ropeworks, Port Glasgow, now a piece of sculpture on a site opposite the works.

PORT GLASGOW, STEAM HAMMER

Port Glasgow, Inverclyde

View from park

When the Gourock Ropeworks in Port Glasgow ceased production in the mid 1970s this steam hammer was retrieved from the workshop and mounted as a landscape feature in public open space on the site of Port Glasgow harbour. The hammer was built by Glen & Ross of Glasgow in 1885, to a patent design by William Rigby, and is typical of very many such tools used in Scottish industry.

PRESTONGRANGE INDUSTRIAL HERITAGE MUSEUM

Prestonpans, East Lothian
Tel: (0131) 653 2904

Open: *April to September, daily*

Admission: *Charges*

Refreshments: *Tea room*

Parking: *Car and coach park*

Disabled access: *Reasonable*

The genesis of a Scottish mining museum was the decision taken in 1954 to save the Cornish pumping engine at Prestongrange Colliery from scrapping, when it reached the end of its useful life. After the colliery itself closed and was dismantled, the engine was retained, looking rather forlorn in a sea of the salt-glazed sewer pipes made by the adjacent fireclay works. In the mid 1960s when serious interest in Scottish industrial archaeology began, David Spence, a retired colliery manager, secured the support of Frank Tindall, Director of Planning in East Lothian County Council in establishing a mining museum with the engine as centrepiece. The former colliery power station was taken over and re-roofed to provide space for machinery displays, and the National Coal Board made interesting specimens available. The beam

The Cornish pumping engine at Prestongrange Industrial Heritage Museum, installed here in 1874 to pump water from under-sea workings.

pumping engine (the only one in Scotland) was restored to good external condition, and the installation of outdoor exhibits began. The steam winding engine from the nearby Newcraighall Colliery was partly re-erected, but has not been completed. Colliery locomotives and rolling stock came from Lady Victoria and other Lothian collieries. These items include a handsome steam crane. A small steel headgear was brought from Littlemill Colliery in Ayrshire and re-erected as a 'shop sign', and more recently some mine cars have added to the atmosphere. The former pithead baths have been adapted as a visitor centre, with displays on coal mining.

Though the bulk of the buildings of the adjacent brick and fireclay pipe works have been demolished, a Hoffman continuous brick kiln and chimney survive to the west of the main site. Apart from the kilns at Dalmellington, this is the only brick kiln preserved in Scotland.

The Scottish Mining Museum expanded in the early 1980s with the addition of the Lady Victoria Colliery at Newtongrange. For more than 10 years the two sites were jointly managed, but in 1992 East Lothian District Council decided to 'go it alone', and the Prestongrange complex is now managed as part of the East Lothian Museums Service. Its policy is to develop the museum to interpret local industries.

PRESTON ISLAND, COAL MINE AND SALTWORKS

Preston Island, Near Valleyfield, Fife

View from shore

Though currently only visible from the old shore line, Preston Island is an industrial site of very considerable interest, and as it is being consolidated with a view to attracting visitors, it seems worth including in this volume. It is an artificial island in the Forth, now embedded in a system of lagoons used for the deposition of fly ash produced by burning pulverised coal in Longannet Power Station. On the island are an engine house for a beam pumping engine, two mineshafts, the upstanding remains of three salt pans, and the shell of a block of houses used by workers. Though there are remains of each of these in other parts of Scotland, nowhere else is there such clear evidence of the integrated coal, which seems to have been characteristic of the Scottish salt industry until it was extinguished by the abolition of the salt tax in 1825 which opened up the Scottish market to cheap English salt. The complex dates from about 1810.

PRESTON MILL

East Linton, East Lothian
Tel: (01620) 860426

Open: *April to September, daily; October, Saturdays and Sundays*

Admission: *Charges*

Refreshments: *None*

Parking: *Good*

Disabled access: *Exterior and ground floor only*

The picturesque qualities of this mill, with its circular kiln, pantiles and reddish sandstone construction, made it sufficiently attractive for The National Trust for Scotland to take it over in the 1960s. Its machinery was brought back into working condition, and the low breast wheel, dating from around 1900, still churns away in the shallow valley of the Tyne. The National Trust for Scotland has long claimed a 17th century date for the mill. There may be parts of the masonry which date from that period, but the bulk of the mill, and certainly the machinery, are not much more than a century old.

Preston Mill, East Linton, with the unusual corn-drying kiln on the left.

RENFREW, MARINE ENGINE AND FORMER ERSKINE FERRY

Renfrew, Renfrewshire

Engine, view from park; ferry, view from street

The burgh of Renfrew has a long history of maritime activity, including shipbuilding and repairing (the latter still active) and trading. The town is locally known for its ferry across the River Clyde to Yoker, now the only one on the river.

There are two relics of this history preserved at Renfrew. The older and smaller is a pair of marine engines on the esplanade. These were built in 1851 in Glasgow by local men A. & J. Inglis, who went on to be noted builders of fast passenger steamers and other smaller vessels at the mouth of the River Kelvin. The engines are from a paddle tug, the *Clyde*, operated for many years by the Clyde Navigation Trust, which for more than 80 years had its maintenance workshops at Renfrew.

The other maritime relic is one of the chain ferries across the Clyde operated by the Clyde Navigation Trust. At one time or another there were three of these, the last being at Renfrew. The steam-propelled chain ferry preserved was built for service at Erskine, a few miles downstream, but was latterly a spare boat at Renfrew. The chain service – in which the boat pulled itself across the river on fixed chains – ceased in 1984, and Renfrew District Council acquired this vessel for preservation. It was the focus of the Council's display at the Glasgow Garden Festival in 1988, and was fitted with a canopy over the vehicle deck for that purpose. The ferry is not open to the public.

The side-lever engines of the paddle tug Clyde at Renfrew. These engines were designed by a local man, then working for the Glasgow firm of A & J Inglis.

ROBERT SMAIL'S PRINTING WORKS, INNERLEITHEN

Innerleithen, Scottish Borders
Tel: (01896) 830206

Open: *Midsummer to October, daily*

Admission: *Charges*

Refreshments: *None*

Parking: *On street nearby*

Disabled access: *Limited*

In Victorian times it was a test of the status of a town that it had at least one printing works. Posters, letterheads, invoices and visiting cards were all necessary to business and personal life, and many medium-sized towns could also boast a newspaper, even if only a weekly or fortnightly one. The Borders woollen town of Innerleithen generated enough business for the Smail family to establish a small printing works, water-powered from the town lade, and at first only a single storey in height. A second storey was added, and eventually electric power installed. When the last of the family retired in the mid 1980s, the building, with its contents, was drawn to the attention of The National Trust for Scotland, which eventually decided to acquire it. The building and machinery have been carefully conserved, and the files of products, business books, fonts of type are all on show to visitors. A waterwheel has been put back, with the gear to raise it out of the water when appropriate. Printing was so much part of the fabric of life in a country town that it is very good to have this tangible reminder of it.

A line of small belt-driven printing presses at Robert Smail's printing works, Innerleithen.

ROYAL MUSEUM OF SCOTLAND (National Museums of Scotland)

Chambers Street, City of Edinburgh
Tel: (0131) 225 7534
Fax: (0131) 226 5949

Open: *Daily*

Admission: *Free*

Refreshments: *Cafeteria*

Parking: *None*

Disabled access: Access and facilities *good*

The Great Exhibition held in the Crystal Palace, London during 1851 proved to be extremely popular and led to the building of many museums and art galleries in Britain. One of these was the Industrial Museum of Scotland, founded in 1854 to establish 'a Museum of the Industry of the world in special relation to Scotland' according to the first Annual Report. This initial aim changed over the years and in 1864 the Industrial Museum was merged with Edinburgh University's Natural History Museum to become the Edinburgh Museum of Science and Art. Two years later, an engineering workshop was established for the purpose of constructing models. Among the first products were scale models of a coal-gas manufacturing plant, winches, cranes and steam hammers. More ambitious projects followed including working models, such as the three-cyclinder compound steam engine from the steamship *Australia* which was completed in 1879. Many fine working models followed.

The range and size of the museum's collections continued to grow and a separate Department of Technology was founded in 1901. On the occasion of the museum's 50th anniversary in 1904 it was granted the title of Royal Scottish Museum. During the ensuing years the transport collection grew as part of the major display themes covering the history of 'Machinery' and later 'Power', rather than as a distinct collection. For example, the development of the petrol engine was closely linked to the motor car, whereas most of the early steam engines were built for industrial use and therefore stationary. Many of the exhibits were cut-away to demonstrate the working principles of the engine or mechanism. For this purpose some excellent working models were produced in the museum's engineering workshop.

In 1985, the Royal Scottish Museum was merged with the National Museum of Antiquities of Scotland to become the National Museums of Scotland, with headquarters at the Royal Museum of Scotland, in Chambers Street, Edinburgh. During the late 1990s a new building was erected on the adjacent site to house the Scottish collections. This has resulted in major rearrangements of the industrial and technological displays. Some transport exhibits may be found integrated into other exhibitions but large parts of the collections will not be available for viewing for some time. Visitors are advised to telephone if they are interested in a specific object or collection. Inspection of items in store can be arranged by prior written appointment. Many of the larger items are stored at The Granton Centre, Edinburgh which is open to the public on advertised days.

ROAD TRANSPORT

The road transport collection is one of the best in Scotland, although it lacks the large public service vehicles which can be seen in the Glasgow **Museum of Transport.**

Of the horse-drawn vehicles, a hearse from the village of Bolton, in East Lothian, is the most interesting. It was purchased second-hand by the Parish in 1783, but the undercarriage was made very much earlier – probably in the mid 17th century as part of a family coach. This being so, it is believed to be the oldest surviving road vehicle in Scotland. In 1993 a significant group of six horse-drawn vehicles were purchased from the well-known collection operated by Scotmid (formerly known as the St Cuthbert's Co-operative Society). Of these, four were built in Scotland.

The well-balanced cycle collection consists of about 60 machines ranging from an 1820 hobby horse to a mountain bike of 1989. But the most significant item is just a front wheel. It came from the first bicycle to be fitted with pneumatic tyres and it covered 3,000 miles without mishap. The inventor, John Boyd Dunlop, presented the wheel to the museum in 1910.

The motorcycle collection contains several interesting early machines and engines, including the prototype Holden four-cylinder motorcycle of 1895 and a rare Edinburgh-built New Gerrard of 1924. The 1930s and 1940s are not well represented, but from 1950 onwards the collection includes many variations from the very small BSA *Winged Wheel* to the large Ariel *Square Four* or Honda CB750 *Dream*. Many of the motorcycles are capable of being operated.

The museum was very fortunate to acquire several early motor cars when the Motor Museum in London closed in 1922. These vehicles retain a very high percentage of original material as they have not suffered the fate of many early motor cars which have been over-restored. The oldest vehicle in the collection is a Léon Bollée motor tricycle of 1895. The Scottish manufacturer, Albion, is represented by a 'Dogcart' of 1900 and three other vehicles. There are a few other Scottish-built cars in this collection but the **Museum of Transport** in Glasgow has a more complete collection of Scottish-built cars. The collecting policy of the old Royal Scottish Museum was to represent the technical development of the motor car, while the National Museum of Antiquities acquired vehicles associated with Scottish country life, including tractors (*see* **Scottish Agricultural Museum**). The combined collection numbers about 20 cars and a similar number of engines, but not all are in display condition. Several cars are on loan to other museums.

RAILWAYS

The museum has one of the two oldest steam locomotives still in existence in the world. *Wylam Dilly* and its almost identical twin *Puffing Billy* were built in 1813, 16 years before Stephenson's more famous *Rocket*. William Hedley designed and built this pair of locomotives to haul coal wagons or 'dillies' from Wylam Colliery to the River Tyne in Northumberland, where they continued working for almost 50 years. *Puffing Billy* is preserved in the Science Museum, London. The story of the development of the steam locomotive was told with working models as full-size locomotives were too large – even for a spacious Victorian building. However, during the 1960s and 70s a number of locomotives were acquired and housed with the growing collection of the Scottish Railway Preservation Society (*see* **Bo'ness and Kinneil Railway**). These included the L.N.E.R. passenger locomotive *Morayshire* of 1928 and several industrial locomotives, both steam and electric. The oldest surviving Scottish-built locomotive in the country, *Ellesmere*, built in Leith in 1861, has been restored and is scheduled to be displayed in the new Museum of Scotland.

SHIPPING

The maritime collections go back to the early days of the museum, to 1857 in fact, when the first ship model was acquired. This was a paddle boat invented in 1823 by Admiral Sir David Milne, and the original register entry explained 'This model represents a method by which it was proposed to rig a ship's boat with paddles, to be employed for towing the ship in calms by manual power'. This rather unusual model came to the museum as part of a large collection of agricultural models presented by the Highland and Agricultural Society of

Scotland. Over the years a collection of ship models and maritime items was built up but these exhibits were usually displayed as part of other collections. For example, the ship models were included in the Engineering Hall. In the 1930s an extension to the museum was built and this included a new display of shipping which was opened in 1938, and closed in the 1980s.

The total collection of ship models consists of about 350 models and is particularly strong in the general history of the sailing ship and in Scottish fishing boats. The collection is very wide-ranging as one would expect from a comprehensive museum. Some of the earliest ship models in the museum are in the collections of Egyptian Antiquities. These are stylised models of boats buried in the tombs of notable people for their use in life after death. The ethnographic collections also include models, such as Native American canoes and Eskimo kayaks, which are featured as part of the way of life of the people concerned.

One of the most interesting sailing ship models in the collection is the Dutch East Indiaman, *D'Bataviase Eeuw*. The model was probably built in 1719 to commemorate the centenary of the founding of Batavia in Java. The hull is particularly fine and has survived remarkably well, but the rigging was extensively restored in the 1930s. Ship models of the Napoleonic period include eight models made by French prisoners-of-war who occupied their time by producing fine models in bone and other scrap materials.

The collection of steam and motor ships includes several very high quality 'builders' models' produced by shipbuilders to advertise their products, ranging from luxury liners to warships or dredgers. Marine engines in the collection include not only very fine working models of steam engines but also several full-size engines including a very early marine gas turbine of 1949 and a high-pressure steam turbine from the *Queen Elizabeth II*. In addition to ship models, the museum has very important collections of lighthouse material and navigational instruments.

AVIATION AND SPACE FLIGHT

The collections of aviation and space flight are displayed at the **Museum of Flight**, East Fortune.

One of the Royal Museum of Scotland's fine collection of locomotive models: LNER Waverley built in 1906. (Upper)

Wylam Dilly built in 1913 and now one of the two oldest surviving locomotives in the world. (Centre)

The hull of this model of a Dutch East Indiaman D'Bataviase Eeuw, was probably built in 1719, but the rigging is of a later date. (Lower)

The pumping windmill at St Monans saltworks, Fife, with the roofed viewing gallery and 'sails' recently installed by Fife Regional Council.

ST MONANS, SALTWORKS

St Monans, Fife
Tel: None

Open: *Exterior, all reasonable times*

Admission: *Exterior viewing free*

Refreshments: *None*

Parking: *Car park in village, footpath to works*

Disabled access: *Very limited*

Salt extraction from seawater was an important Scottish industry from the 17th century. It was most prominent on the Forth and Clyde estuaries, where coal seams outcropped near the surface and where demand for salt for domestic and industrial purposes was greatest. The saltworks at St Monans, constructed in the mid 18th century was one of the larger works, with its associated coal pits and wagon ways. All that now survives above ground is the stump of a windmill used to pump up seawater to the salt pans, and lower courses of the range of pan houses in which the water was evaporated to produce salt. Fife Regional Council has consolidated

the windmill stump, created a viewing platform on top, and put back an indication of what the sails might have been like. One of the pan houses was excavated in 1985, and there have been recent excavations of other parts of the site. This is an industry where much can be learned by excavation, and the site will repay a series of visits.

SALTCOATS, BEAM ENGINE HOUSE

Saltcoats, North Ayrshire

View from park

Now in the care of North Ayrshire Council, this ruined engine house is the only significant above-ground evidence of the once notable coal industry of this area. One of the first steam engines in Scotland, of the primitive Newcomen type, was installed in 1719 to pump water from the pits, and this engine house is, according to tradition, where it was sited. It now stands in a public open space.

The consolidated ruin, at Saltcoats, of an early beam pumping engine house, reputed to be the site of one of the first steam engines in Scotland. This was a Newcomen engine installed in 1719.

SCOTTISH AGRICULTURAL MUSEUM
(National Museums of Scotland)

Ingliston, City of Edinburgh
Tel: (0131) 333 2674
Fax: (0131) 333 2674

The Scottish Agricultural Museum at Ingliston, near Edinburgh.

Open: *Every day April to September; weekdays, October to March*

Admission: *Free*

Refreshments: *Tea room*

Parking: *Car park*

Disabled access: *Access and facilities good*

The Scottish Agricultural Museum is housed in a modern building on the Royal Highland Showground about 7 miles (11 km) west of Edinburgh. The aim of the museum is to present the old trades and skills of the countryside, especially the many Scottish inventions which improved farming methods. A special exhibition is held every year to explore a different aspect of Scottish country life. A vast archive of photographs includes many illustrations of rural industries and travel and transport in Scotland. Requests to see archive material or objects in store must be made in writing.

Agriculture has always been an important industry in Scotland although it is often overshadowed by the heavy industries. In the 18th and early 19th centuries, Scotland was in the forefront of European agricultural development. The museum features some of the Scottish inventions from this period, sometimes with contemporary models. Examples are: Small's swing plough, Bell's reaper and Meikle's threshing machine, including the oldest surviving example in the world dating from 1804. An important working exhibit, which is occasionally demonstrated at fairs and shows, is a Clayton and Shuttleworth combine harvester *c.*1932 which is probably the oldest working combine harvester in the world.

The museum has a very good collection of about 15 tractors, many in working condition, but some awaiting restoration. Probably the most important example is one built by John Wallace (Glasgow) Ltd., in 1919, which is the only tractor designed and built in Scotland. This makes an interesting comparison with the International *Junior* of the same date.

SCOTTISH CYCLE MUSEUM

Drumlanrig Castle, Thornhill, Dumfries & Galloway
Tel: (01368) 850226

Open: *Late April to September*

Charges: *To Country Park*

Refreshments: *In Country Park*

Parking: *(Country Park)*

Disabled access: *Access good, facilities nearby*

This is probably the largest collection of cycles in Scotland, consisting of over 100 machines – although not all of them are on display at present. The collection was brought together by Alex Brown and is administered by the Scottish Cycle Museum Trust.

Drumlanrig Castle is a very appropriate location for a cycle museum because the generally accepted inventor of the pedal-cycle, Kirkpatrick Macmillan, worked on the estate for the Duke of Buccleuch. Macmillan was a blacksmith and lived nearby at Courthill, in a cottage with a smithy attached. Having tried out a hobby-horse, propelled like a scooter, Macmillan devised a cycle powered by pedals which were connected by links and cranks to the rear wheel. His successful machine was built in about 1840 and several other people copied his design. In 1842 Macmillan cycled to Glasgow and back, a distance of about 130 miles (209 km). Unfortunately, his cycle did not survive but the museum have built a replica, and re-created a smithy. A period shop window has also been re-created.

With the limited accommodation available, about 80 cycles are on display, plus many other small items associated with cycling, from an oil can to a picnic set. However, the cycles are the main interest and there are examples of all the milestones in the development of the cycle, such as the Ordinary or 'penny farthing', and the 'safety' bicycle. Many of these can be seen in other collections but it is doubtful if any other collection can match the Scottish-built machines on display. There is a rare Melvin built about 1905, a 1936 racing cycle built in Hamilton by E. & S. Worrall, and several Glasgow-built models.

Just a few miles to the south is the picturesque Dalswinton Loch on which William Symington demonstrated his first steamboat in 1788, with Robert Burns as a passenger. The engine from this boat is preserved in the Science Museum, London.

SCOTTISH FISHERIES MUSEUM

St Ayles, Harbourhead, Anstruther, Fife
Tel: (01333) 310628

Open: *Daily, all year*

Admission: *Charges*

Refreshments: *Tea room*

Parking: *Public car park nearby*

Disabled access: *Ramps, toilet*

The Scottish Fisheries Museum is one of the most attractive museums in the country, being housed in a group of historic buildings around a cobbled courtyard, overlooking Anstruther harbour. The buildings, known as 'St Ayles', have been associated with fishermen and fishing for centuries. Before being taken over by the museum they were used by a ships chandler; the 'gallowses', on which nets were hung to dry, survive. More recently, the museum has acquired the nearby premises which housed Smith and Hutton's boatyard. This is being developed to display the museum's collection of small vessels and demonstrate how they were built.

The museum was set up by a local Trust and opened for the first time in 1969 with modest displays. As the buildings were restored, new displays were prepared and the quality of the work was recognized by several awards including a Civic Trust Award, an Architectural Heritage Year Award and, in 1976, the Museum of the Year Award for Scotland.

The fishing theme embraces both transport and industry. Initially, models were used to show the variety of fishing boats used by Scottish fishermen, but in 1975 the first actual deep-sea fishing boat was acquired and several more followed. As Anstruther is one of a number of fishing ports on the Fife coast, there has always been a keen local interest in the

Anstruther harbour with the Scottish Fisheries Museum buildings and the hull of the 'Zulu' fishing boat Research *(LK62).*

museum and volunteers have made a great contribution in all aspects of its work. Local fishermen and their families have provided many of the objects on display, and retired fishermen have helped by talking to visitors, especially school parties, and bringing the museum to life.

THE FISHING INDUSTRY

The Museum covers many aspects of the fishing industry from modern technology back to the great days of sail and the fisher lassies who gutted the herring. In those early days there were about ten jobs ashore for every job on board a fishing boat. The fisherfolk were a very close-knit community who had to face hard work and tragedies to survive. The museum has a *Memorial to Scottish Fishermen Lost at Sea.*

There are displays devoted to the methods of catching fish with models to show how the various nets and lines were used, together with actual lobster pots, harpoons for whaling, and modern sonic scanners used to find the shoals of fish. Land-based trades include boat building, sail making and coopering (making barrels to transport the fish). In one of the oldest buildings on the site, dating from the 16th century, there is a reconstruction of a fisherman's home of about 1900 and a net-loft. The displays include many figures in costumes from the museum's large costume collection; there are also many photographs and paintings.

BOAT COLLECTION

Scottish fishing boats usually carried two masts each with a lug sail. There were three basic hull designs: the 'Fifie' with vertical stem and stern posts; the 'Skaffie' with rounded stem, acutely raked stern posts, and the compromise 'Zulu' with a Fifie bow and Skaffie stern. The museum has many models but the real thing is far more impressive. A Fifie called *Reaper* which had been built in 1902, and later much modified, was restored to its original configuration as a herring drifter. *Reaper* is usually moored near the museum, but sometimes is away on voyages – she has appeared in several films. Then followed a 'Zulu' built in Banff in 1903 and called *Research,* and a relatively modern boat built in 1957 named *Radiation* used for 'great-line' fishing. This latter boat is of particular interest as it was built at the local shipyard in Anstruther. Due to her size, *Radiation* can be seen in Victoria Dock, Dundee. The museum has several smaller boats, including one unusual craft, a yawl named *Jim* which was used for racing by coal-miners from Dysart, near Kirkcaldy.

Recent acquisitions include *Lively Hope*, a ring-net herring boat of the 1930s, and a Scottish sea-going salmon cobble, *Jubilee.*

SCOTTISH INDUSTRIAL RAILWAY CENTRE

Minnivey, near Dalmellington, East Ayrshire

Tel: (01292) 313579

Open: *Weekends in summer*

Admission: *Charges*

Refreshments: *Tea room*

Parking: *Car park*

Disabled access: *Fair*

The small but energetic and enterprising Ayrshire Railway Preservation Group has worked since 1974 to provide a focus for railway preservation in south west Scotland. Greatly to its credit it has focused sharply on railways and industry, and has now formed the Scottish Industrial Railway Centre. This is not the place to discuss the role of transport in industry, but it is to mention the splendid collection of Scottish-made locomotives and rolling stock in the care of the group. These include four- and six-wheeled steam locomotives by Andrew Barclay Sons & Co. Ltd. of Kilmarnock, Scotland's foremost industrial locomotive builders, and diesel locomotives by the same maker. Wagons almost certainly of Scottish manufacture are also represented. The associations of some of the other equipment are also relevant. There is a steam crane

from R. & J. Tennent's rolling mill roll works in Coatbridge, and locomotives from British Steel and ICI as well as from the National Coal Board (British Coal), and vans used in connection with whisky blending. Perhaps the most compellingly important aspect of the collection is that it contains both locomotives and wagons used on the local industrial lines. The group is planning to work trains through from the Minnivey site to the Doon Valley Heritage site at Dunaskin.

SCOTTISH MARITIME MUSEUM, IRVINE

Irvine, North Ayrshire

Tel: (01294) 278283

Open: *April to October, daily*

Admission: *Charges*

Refreshments: *Tea room*

Parking: *Car park and street parking*

Disabled access: *Good, except to vessels*

The Scottish Maritime Museum is the triumphant survivor from a number of more or less visionary schemes devised from the early 1970s for sites including Queen's Dock, the Govan Graving Docks,

Industrial steam exhibits at Minnivey, with a locomotive from the local colliery system on the right and a fireless locomotive from Ardrossan Oil Refinery on the left.

The puffer Spartan *at the Scottish Maritime Museum, Irvine. It was the gift of this vessel by the Glenlight Shipping Company that triggered the establishment of the museum.*

The tug Garnock, built by George Brown of Greenock, for the Irvine Harbour Company, and now preserved by the Scottish Maritime Museum.

The sailing vessel Carrick on the slipway at the Scottish Maritime Museum, showing the elegant underwater shape of the last of the wool clippers.

and Yorkhill Quay, Glasgow, Bowling Harbour and Greenock. The main factors in creating a maritime museum at Irvine were the establishment of the West of Scotland Boat Museum Association, and the interest of Irvine New Town Development Corporation in improving the near-derelict harbour area, blighted by decaying residues of manufacturing industry.

Persuaded that a museum devoted solely to small craft would not have enough appeal to attract large-scale funding, both major partners agreed to the founding in 1985 of the Scottish Maritime Museum

Trust (Irvine), the Scottish title only being allowed after assurances of the genuinely national objectives of the organisation. The Development Corporation has undertaken a major programme of upgrading the quayside area, provided pontoons for the mooring of vessels, financed the building of a small museum, and most recently been a partner with other funding agencies in relocating the pioneering cast-iron framed marine engine works from Alexander Stephen & Sons Linthouse shipyard in Glasgow. Meantime, the museum has collected an internationally-important collection of shipbuilding tools and a very fine group of full-sized boats and small ships, including the Marquis of Bute's *Lady Guilford* of 1818, the *Kyles* – an ancient iron coaster – and the Greenock-built tug *Garnock*, as well as yachts (including the steam yacht *Carola*), fishing boats, rowing boats and launches. A tenement flat close to the harbour has been fitted out as a shipyard worker's house of the early 20th century. To back up these major items a large collection of books, photographs, other documentary material, models and small objects has been assembled, fully justifying the 'Scottish' in the title.

At present, a visitor to the museum can approach it by road or rail. If coming by road the first section encountered is the pontoons with the *Spartan,* lifeboats and other small craft. Visitors can board the *Spartan,* and the lifeboats. The cramped crew's quarters on the *Spartan* are a revelation – and these are an improvement on those in earlier puffers. At high tide and on certain days a ferry will take visitors from the pontoons to the slipway and boatshop museums further up river. The slipway is used for repairing both historic and non-historic craft and often gives visitors an opportunity to see techniques of repairing both wooden and metal craft. On show in the slipway area are an RAF rescue boat, moored during the Second World War to provide a refuge for ditched airmen, and some items of machinery, including a hand winch and a steam hammer. At an adjacent berth is the tug *Garnock*. The boatshop museum was originally intended as a workshop for the construction or repair of small wooden craft, but in the absence of other display space is used for temporary exhibitions. It also houses the museum shop. Beyond this building are the ancient coaster *Kyles,* and the wool clipper *Carrick* (ex *City of Adelaide*), which was rescued from a watery grave in Glasgow, and which is now slipped for repair.

The museum workshops and offices are in Gottries Road, which is about a hundred metres from the harbour, housed in a building formerly part of a forge noted for rigging blocks. Immediately to the east the most exciting development is taking place: the re-erection and fitting out of the Linthouse engine shop. An exhibit in its own right, with its superb cast-iron frame and massive open timber roof, the Linthouse building will house a wide range of facilities for visitors as well as both permanent and temporary exhibitions. When this is complete the museum will take its place as one of the United Kingdom's leading museums.

SCOTTISH MINING MUSEUM

Newtongrange, Midlothian
Tel: (0131) 663 7519

Open: *April to September, daily*

Admission: *Charges*

Refreshments: *Tea room*

Parking: *Car and coach park*

Disabled access: *Limited*

Coalmining was historically one of Scotland's most important industries and it is not surprising that it figures largely in museum and preserved site provision. The first mining museum in Scotland was at **Prestongrange** and when in 1981 the opportunity offered by the closure of Lady Victoria Colliery was taken up, the intention was that the two sites should become one integrated museum, as what they had to offer was complementary. This approach worked for a number of years, but was terminated in 1992, when East Lothian District Council resolved to run Prestongrange as a part of its local museum service.

Lady Victoria was chosen as Scotland's preserved colliery partly because it had the largest and finest steam winding engine in the country. This was one of the first group of industrial monuments in Scotland to be scheduled as Ancient Monuments, and the scheduling was the key to the preservation of the whole site. The colliery was one of the first large deep mines in Scotland, sunk to the bottom of the Lothian coal basin, and was designed for a long life. It was sunk during the 1890s, and embodied the best practice of the time. Soon after completion, the use of electricity underground became practical, and a power station was built. This was later extended.

The north end of the Lady Victoria Colliery, Newtongrange, now the centrepiece of the Scottish Mining Museum.

The boilerhouse at Lady Victoria Colliery, used to supply steam to the great winding engine of 1894, the largest in Scotland.

The development of coal washing techniques early this century resulted in the addition of a washer, and in the 1960s this was replaced by a dense-medium washer, which also dealt with coal from Easthouses Colliery. These are all still extant, though the power houses were abandoned when mains electricity became available, and the generating plant was removed. The colliery is certainly one of the finest 19th-century coal mines surviving, and probably the finest.

A visit to the museum starts with the colliery office, where lay figures wired for sound tell the story of a miner, his family and relations with his employers in a dramatic and immediate way. From this introduction, visitors are taken on tours of those parts of the colliery currently safe for visitors. The giant winding engine made by Grant, Ritchie of Kilmarnock in 1894 is shown with electric motor drive to the drum. From the engine house the tour passes into the pithead area, with hutch run and tipplers, below the headframes. Planning is under way for the repair of the complex to allow visitors to follow the route the coal took to railway wagons for despatch to customers. In the meantime, visitors can view an exhibition in the old power station, where a permanent exhibit is 'Old Ben', a rotative beam engine last used at Highhouse Colliery, Auchinleck, and said to have been originally constructed as a Newcomen engine. Transport items in the collection include underground diesel and electric locomotives and rolling stock and a saddle tank locomotive and wagons.

SCOTTISH MUSEUM OF WOOL TEXTILES, WALKERBURN

Tweedvale Mill, Walkerburn, Scottish Borders
Tel: (01896) 870619

Open: *April to October, Monday to Saturday*

Admission: *Free*

Refreshments: *Coffee shop*

Parking: *Car and coach park*

Disabled access: *Good*

This rather grandiose title reflects more the aspirations of its founder than the practical realisation of his dreams. Henry Ballantine, a director of the family firm that owned the Walkerburn mills, saw the disappearance of old technologies from the woollen industry in Scotland, and collected old machinery with a view to displaying it in museum conditions. Unfortunately, the death of the founder halted the idea in its tracks, and retrenchment in the woollen trade followed. The museum now takes the form of a few small displays in a wool shop, a long way short of Henry Ballantine's vision.

SHAWBOST, HORIZONTAL MILL

Shawbost, Isle of Lewis, Western Isles

Tel: None

Open: *Accessible at all reasonable hours*

Admission: *Free*

Refreshments: *None*

Parking: *None formal*

Disabled access: *Very limited*

The horizontal mill, sometimes known as the 'black' mill in Lewis, was fairly common in that part of the 'Long Island'. This example on an oval plan, and built from water-worn boulders, was reconstructed in the late 1960s by local schoolchildren from a much-decayed structure, using photographic evidence of comparable examples as a guide. It was reconditioned in the early 1990s.

The little 'black' or horizontal mill at Shawbost, Lewis, reconstructed by local school children in the 1960s.

SHETLAND CROFT HOUSE MUSEUM, HORIZONTAL MILL

Voe, Dunrossness, Shetland

Tel: (01595) 695057

Open: *May to September, daily*

Admission: *Charges*

Refreshments: *None*

Parking: *Good*

Disabled access: *Fair*

Now part of the farm museum run by Shetland Council, this horizontal mill was one of a pair; the other is now a store. This type of mill was common in Shetland, and the Southvoe mills with their thatched roofs are very typical, as is their location on a small fast-flowing stream. The mills are rather smaller, and less externally altered, than the Click Mill at Dounby.

The horizontal mill at the Shetland Croft House Museum, Southvoe. It is mechanically similar to the Shawbost mill, though externally very different.

SHETLAND MUSEUM

Lower Hillhead, Lerwick, Shetland
Tel: (01595) 695057
Fax: (01595) 696729

The Shetland Museum's Ness yoal Maggie (right) sailing off Virkie, Dunrossness.

Open: *All year, Monday to Saturday*

Admission: *Free*

Refreshments: *None*

Parking: *Car park*

Disabled access: *Access and facilities good*

Shetland has an impressive number of museums and visitor centres; 15 are listed in one very useful joint brochure. Many of the museums are housed in historic buildings such as the **Böd of Gremista** and the **Pier House**. In contrast, the Shetland Museum and Library occupy a purpose-built building erected in 1966.

The theme of the collections and displays is *Life in Shetland Throughout the Ages*. This theme is displayed in three sections: *Archaeology* which covers Neolithic to medieval times; *Folklife/Historical* which deals with the pre-industrial past and, finally, *Maritime Matters*. There are several items relating to industry and transport in the second section including two ploughs and other farming items, peat cutting and gathering implements, and the saddles with their panniers

used by Shetland ponies. There is a restored pony stud farm a short distance from Lerwick and the travel directions read 'Access is by car ferry from Lerwick to Bressay and then by inflatable boat across a narrow sound (weather permitting)'. This clearly emphasises the important part played by the sea in Shetland everyday life, including both transport and industry.

The maritime gallery includes figureheads from the days of sail; one from a German brig wrecked in 1877. There are several relics from wrecks emphasising the dangers of sea travel in these northern waters. In fact, there are so few trees on Shetland that some of the locally-built boats and furniture were manufactured from the wood recovered from wrecks or from driftwood.

One very notable miniature model represents the schooner-rigged *Matchless*, a popular passenger packet which plied between Leith and Lerwick from 1846 to 1882. The steamship era made travel to and from Shetland much more reliable and several of the vessels used are represented by models. There are three builder's models of ships built for the North of Scotland Company covering the period from 1887 to

1977. Another very fine model is that of the lighthouse tender *Pole Star* on loan from the Commissioners of Northern Lights who operate the lighthouses around the coast of Scotland.

Shetland was not a base for the Arctic whaling industry but local sailors were recruited by the whaling companies, and some of their relics and stories are presented in the displays. There was a very important fishing industry in Shetland using open boats operating from the numerous beaches of the islands. There are several excellent models on display including a Ness yoal, a Fair Isle yoal and a sixern made by the late John Shewan, a local model-maker who made models for most of the ship-model collections in Britain. The museum also has a full-size Ness yoal which has been restored and is sailed for special events. Boats from different islands varied in detail design and the museum's example came from Dunrossness, near Sumburgh.

SKERRYVORE LIGHTHOUSE MUSEUM

Hynish, Isle of Tiree, Argyll & Bute
Tel: c/o L. MacFarlane (018792) 20691

Open: *Every day*

Admission: *Free*

Refreshments: *None*

Parking: *Car park*

Disabled access: *Access difficult*

This museum is one of the smallest in the British Isles: it is housed in the former signal tower for the Skerryvore Lighthouse which is some 10 miles (16 km) out in the Atlantic. Signal towers were used to send visual signals when a lighthouse was within sight of the shore. The use of radio made the signal towers redundant, and the keepers suffered a similar fate when automatic lights were installed.

The Skerryvore Lighthouse was built in 1843, on an isolated rock in the Atlantic by one of the famous Stevenson family of civil engineers. Robert built the Bell Rock Lighthouse (*see* **Arbroath Museum**) and his son Alan built the one on Skerryvore. Alan's brothers David and Thomas were both engineers but Thomas's son, despite visiting many lighthouses, became a writer – Robert Louis Stevenson.

The museum tells the story of the building of the Skerryvore Lighthouse, which was a particularly difficult operation due to the dreadful weather conditions. Hynish was used as the base for the construction and manning of the lighthouse. There is a telescope which enables visitors to see the lighthouse – weather permitting. Incidentally, the museum was founded in 1985 and during its first year it had over 2,000 visitors – on an island with a population of only 790.

The Hebridean Trust who set up the museum have also restored the harbour with its unique flushing system to keep it free from silting up. This system was designed by Stevenson when he built the lighthouse, and utilized a fresh-water reservoir from which water could be released and wash away any build-up of sand. The Trust re-enacted the flushing process in 1985 for the first time in 100 years and proved that it worked.

SMITH ART GALLERY AND MUSEUM, STIRLING

40 Albert Place, Dumbarton Road, Stirling
Tel: (01786) 471917
Fax: (01786) 432056

Open: *All year, closed Mondays*

Admission: *Free*

Refreshments: *Cafeteria*

Parking: *Car park*

Disabled access: *Assisted access, facilities*

'Stirling museum falling victim to decay' said a newspaper headline in 1972. The museum was then 98 years old and its chances of reaching 100 were not good. It had been founded by a rich benefactor Thomas Stuart Smith, but his endowment was not able to cope with inflation and escalating maintenance costs. In 1973, support from Stirling District Council, Central Regional Council, and the Friends of the Smith saved the day and it is now a museum Stirling can be proud of.

For a number of years the museum featured temporary exhibitions – especially ones involving local people, but there is now a permanent exhibition entitled 'A Job Well Done: Stirling People at Work 1750–1990'. The presentation concentrates on social history rather than a history of industries or transport. It is well presented and each distinct section includes many relevant artifacts. There are sections on 'Spinning and Weaving', 'The Industrial Revolution 1840–1914', 'Mining', 'The Railway, Shops and Tourists' and 'Old and New Industries'. Finally, there is an Activity Area with videos, slides and photographs. There is also a very easy-to-follow *Script* of the exhibition aimed at teachers bringing school parties, and visitors in general.

SPRINGBURN MUSEUM

Atlas Square, Ayr Street, City of Glasgow
Tel: (0141) 557 1405

Open: *Every day, Sundays p.m.*

Admission: *Free*

Refreshments: *None*

Parking: *Car park*

Disabled access: *Access good, no toilet*

Springburn is on the northern side of Glasgow about 3 miles (5 km) from the city centre. In the 1820s it was a small mining and cotton-weaving village, but some 60 years later it was the largest centre of steam locomotive building in Europe. The four large railway works employed 9,000 men and the locomotives they built were widely used throughout Britain, and exported to 60 countries worldwide. By the 1960s this once great industry was all but dead.

Springburn Museum was opened in 1986 as a community museum and, as such, does not have large permanent displays. Its frequently changing exhibitions and events reflect all aspects of the life of the community, in the present as well as the past. These have ranged from 'Springburn Mothers' to the 'History of the Cowlairs Works from 1841 to 1966'.

In addition to photographs, archives and ephemera, the museum has two railway models. One is a Caledonian Railway *Dunalastair II* class of steam locomotive built in their St Rollox Works, Springburn at the turn of the century. The second model is of a coach built by the North British Railway's Cowlairs Works. In contrast, the museum does own one of the largest steam locomotives in

A display of measuring and other small tools used in locomotive building in Springburn. (Above left)

A large 4-8-2 locomotive built by the North British Locomotive Company in Springburn 1938-9 being loaded at Glasgow Docks. (Left)

Britain. This is a double-locomotive with a single boiler, known as a 'Garratt' (after the inventor Herbert W. Garratt). It was built in 1956 by the North British Locomotive Company at their Hyde Park Works in Springburn for South African Railways. It returned to Scotland in 1990, but as there was nowhere to display it at Springburn, it was lent to the **Summerlee Heritage Park** at Coatbridge.

SS SIR WALTER SCOTT, TROSSACHS PIER

Trossachs Pier, nearest town Callander, Stirling

Tel: (0141) 355 5333

Open: *April to September, daily*

Admission: *Charges*

Refreshments: *Cafeteria on board*

Parking: *Car and coach park*

Disabled access: *With difficulty*

Included because unlike the paddle steamer *Waverley* she never strays from her native water, this little vessel is the only screw passenger steamer regularly operating in Scottish waters. She was built in 1900 by the Dumbarton shipbuilders William Denny & Brothers and has her original triple-expansion engines. Loch Katrine, on which she plies, has supplied Glasgow with water since the 1850s,

and the necessity for a clean catchment has kept its environs unspoilt. A steamship is the ideal vessel for this romantic loch, linked forever with Sir Walter Scott's poem 'The Lady of the Lake'. The ship plies regularly in the summer months, adding a touch of Victorian elegance to the picturesque scenery.

STEWARTRY MUSEUM

Saint Mary Street, Kirkcudbright, Dumfries & Galloway

Tel: (01557) 331643

Fax: (01557) 330005

Open: *March to October, Monday to Saturday; June to September, Sunday (p.m.); Winter, Saturday only*

Admission: *Charges*

Refreshments: *At Tolbooth Art Centre (nearby)*

Parking: *Car park*

Disabled access: *Limited, no toilet*

Before the introduction of Regions and Districts there was a county of Kirkcudbrightshire which was also known as the Stewartry, because it was once under the jurisdiction of a Royal Steward. The museum was for many years run by the Stewartry

The screw steamer Sir Walter Scott, built in 1900 by William Denny & Bros., Dumbarton, which plies in summer on Loch Katrine, as she has done for nearly a century.

Museum Association but it is now operated by the Dumfries & Galloway Museums Service.

Most of the transport exhibits relate to the sea, although there is one early motor car engine; this is from a Benz car imported from Germany in 1897 and was the first private car to run in the area. The Shipping Gallery has on display many paintings, prints and photographs illustrating shipping associated with the ports along the southern coast of Dumfries and Galloway. There are several hull half-models and a model of the ferry boat which plied across the River Dee at Kirkcudbright, until a bridge was built in 1868. Other displays feature local lifeboats and their stations, and a colourful character born in Kirkcudbright called John Paul Jones, who became an American naval hero and fought against the British in the 1770s. Later, in 1790, he became an Admiral in the Russian Navy. More information on Jones can be found in the Tolbooth Art Centre nearby – a building in which he was imprisoned briefly in 1770.

Industrial exhibits include small items representing local crafts and trades, such as tools and agricultural implements.

Plaque from the first bridge over the River Dee at Kirkcudbright, now outside the Stewartry Museum, Kirkcudbright.

STRANRAER MUSEUM

55 George Street, Stranraer, Dumfries & Galloway
Tel: (01776) 705088

Open: *All year, Monday to Saturday*

Admission: *Free*

Refreshments: *None*

Parking: *Public car park nearby*

Disabled access: *Access and facilities good*

Stranraer Museum was until April 1996 the headquarters of the Wigtown District Museum Service which is also responsible for the Castle of St John in Stranraer and the Wigtown Museum. Wigtown was the county town until local government reorganisation in 1975 and the museum displays include a wide range of standard weights and measures from the early 1700s.

The museum is housed in the Old Town Hall and has been upgraded and adapted for disabled visitors. Agriculture is one of the principal industries of the area and this is well presented with an historical account covering 6,000 years. An important exhibit is the Chilcarroch plough – the only surviving example of a plough which was widely used in Scotland prior to the agricultural revolution of the 1700s. Another display covers the specialisation on dairy farming and creameries in more recent times. There is also a collection of spinning wheels, looms, early cycles and a tractor which are not on display but may be seen by appointment. A programme of temporary exhibitions is pursued every year in the main gallery, which may use reserve material.

Stranraer is a well-known port for travellers to Northern Ireland, but less well-known as the home of two famous travellers to the Arctic. The museum has a room devoted to the Polar explorer Sir John Ross and his nephew Sir James Clark Ross, who also led the first British Antarctic expedition in 1839.

STRATHSPEY RAILWAY

Aviemore Speyside Station, Dalfaber Road,
Aviemore, Highland

Tel: (01479) 810725

Fax: (01479) 831279

Open: *Easter to October.*
NB. Not every day, check by telephone

Admission: *Fare for train ride*

Refreshments: *On trains*

Parking: *Car parks*

Disabled access: *Visitors by appointment*

When the former British Railways line from Aviemore to Boat of Garten was reopened by a group of enthusiastic volunteers in 1978 it became Scotland's first full-scale preserved railway. The Strathspey Railway Company had been founded seven years earlier and much hard work was needed to achieve their aim of a steam railway working in the Highlands. Now with a few paid staff and many volunteers, services are operated from Easter to October. The five-mile (8 km) journey between Aviemore and Boat of Garten takes 20 minutes and passes along the pleasant countryside of the Strathspey with mountains in the background. Passengers can start their journey at Aviemore, or Boat of Garten Station where there is a small museum containing archives and small objects such as lamps and crockery. It is hoped to extend the line beyond Boat of Garten to Grantown-on-Spey in the future and a replica station building has been constructed at Broomhill – some 4 miles (6 km) north of Boat of Garten.

RAILWAY COLLECTION

This is a working vintage railway rather than a conventional museum so visitors have the advantage of seeing the trains in action, but the disadvantage of not having all the locomotives and rolling stock on view all the time. Also, some of the items are on loan and, therefore, may be removed or changed.

The normal complement of steam locomotives is about a dozen, the oldest of which is the Caledonian Railway No. 828 built in 1899. The largest locomotive is LMS 'Black Five' No. 5025 which is on loan from a private owner. 'Black Fives' were a common sight on Scottish main lines for many years. Most of the other steam locomotives are former industrial locomotives from a variety of sources: collieries, distilleries, a power station, etc. Although most of the passenger services are steam-hauled, occasionally the company do use one of their larger diesel locomotives. Most of the diesels are small industrial locomotives from the 1950s and used for shunting, but the 1959 Class 08 diesel-hydraulic has been used to haul passenger trains. The Class 27 D5394 sees regular use on Royal Scotsman passenger trains and works trains.

To operate regular passenger services requires a considerable stock of carriages. The Strathspey Railway have about 30, of which those built in the 1950s are in the majority. Nevertheless, there are some historic carriages such as a Highland Railway brake van built *c.*1870, a Great North of Scotland Railway composite coach of 1896, and an 1898 luggage van also used by the same company. Many of the 20 wagons and three cranes are used for maintenance work and other useful services, particularly keeping the track in good order. One of the cranes dates back to 1905 when it was used by the Caledonian Railway. Many of the wagons are painted in the livery of the industrial users who presented them to the Strathspey Railway.

Boat of Garten Station, dating from 1904 and now doubling as station and museum for the Strathspey Railway.

STROMNESS MUSEUM, ORKNEY

52 Alfred Street, Stromness, Orkney
Tel: (01856) 850025

Open: *All year, Monday to Saturday;*
May to September, Sunday

Admission: *Charges*

Refreshments: *None*

Parking: *Car park*

Disabled access: *Limited to ground floor, no toilet*

Although the Stromness Museum is owned and administered by the Orkney Natural History Society Museum Trust (founded in 1837), its displays are on a much broader base. It has a collective policy with the Orkney Museums Service which operates from the Tankerness House Museum in Kirkwall.

Stromness Museum's two main themes are natural history and the sea. There are model ships including fishing boats, sailing ships and steamers. Travel by sea was the only way to travel between the islands, or to the rest of the world until air travel was introduced in the 1930s. Other displays feature fishing, whaling, lifeboats, lighthouses and boat-building.

The museum has recently opened a new extension, having incorporated an adjoining building, formerly the home of a Stromness pilot. In the 17th and 18th centuries, Stromness was an international port-of-call for Atlantic-bound shipping. In the 1820s it still had a greater number of pilots than any other Scottish port. The Pilot's House extension has exhibitions on Orkney sail traders, deep sea sailors, Arctic whaling, and the Moravian mission ships which called annually on their way to Labrador.

Another display features the strong links with the Hudson's Bay Company in Canada as many Orcadians, including the Arctic explorer Dr John Rae, worked for the Company and their ships often sailed into Stromness. Sir John Franklin sailed out of Stromness in 1845 on his ill-fated quest to find the 'North West Passage' to the far east. This, and other stories of Arctic exploration, are told in an exhibition.

The huge natural harbour of Scapa Flow is probably Orkney's most famous landmark. During two World Wars it was one of the Royal Navy's most important bases, and at the end of World War I the scuttling of the German fleet made headlines round the world. Later, the salvaging of some of these warships for scrap became quite a local industry. The story of Scapa Flow is told with photographs, documents, and relics from the wrecks.

Farming on Orkney is covered at two of the other museums, at Kirbister and Corrigall. The latter includes horse-drawn vehicles, a grain-drying kiln and a loom. Nearby is the 'Click Mill', with the only surviving example of an Orcadian horizontal water mill.

SUMMERLEE HERITAGE PARK, COATBRIDGE

Coatbridge, North Lanarkshire
Tel: (01236) 431 261

Open: *All year, daily, except Christmas and New Year*

Admission: *Free*

Refreshments: *Tea room*

Parking: *Car park*

Disabled access: *Excellent*

The Summerlee Heritage Park was very clearly a 1980s project, born of the need for urban regeneration in Monklands District, and the availability of labour under the various job creation schemes run by the Manpower Services Commission. The Scottish Development Agency was a prime mover in this scheme, which probably owed its conception to the abortive ideas for steel museums at Victoria Works, Coatbridge, and on a national scale at Glengarnock. Summerlee, as originally envisaged, was something of a themepark, with attractions such as a steam railway and canal boats, as part of the reclamation of an area of derelict land close to the centre of Coatbridge. A design study was commissioned from land use

Repairing a boat in the recreated boatshop at Summerlee. (Right)

A huge Beyer Garratt locomotive built by the North British Locomotive Company in Springburn for South African Railways. On loan from Springburn Museum. (Below)

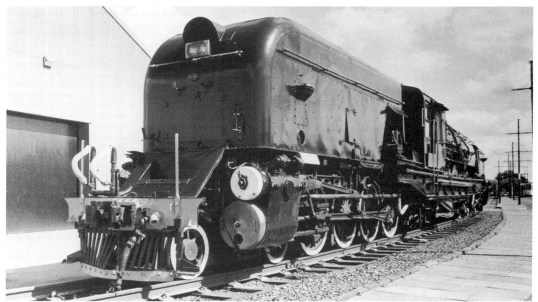

consultants, and at the discussion stage the museum part of the concept was toughened up, with the vision that in default of any other initiative Summerlee could become *the* museum of the heavy industries (other than shipbuilding and coal mining) in west central Scotland.

The models on which Summerlee is based include Beamish, the Blists Hill part of the Ironbridge Gorge Museum and the Black Country Museum at Dudley. It shares with all of these the concept of the 'open air museum', with Beamish and the Black Country Museum a tramway, with the Black Country Museum a canal, but it has its own distinctive features, including the excavated remains of the Summerlee Ironworks, and a large covered area, built as a crane works after the Second World War, which is used for heavy exhibits and other displays. The first phase of the museum's

development centred on the covered area, which has had its office block demolished, and the gap built up in traditional red and white brick. The north end walls have been glazed to give a very effective display area. The excavation of the ironworks was begun at the same time, and the tramway quickly followed.

The momentum of development was dramatically slowed down when the Manpower Services Commission was wound up and replaced by the Training Agency. In an area of high unemployment, such as Monklands, the local politicians found this hard to accept, and in the event Monklands District Council declined to participate in Employment Training. Instead the Council voted to pay for the permanent staffing of the museum, stipulating at the same time that as a local authority museum, albeit run by a Trust, admission should be free. The effect has been

A steam day at Summerlee in 1994, with a privately-owned Robey steam roller passing the two steelworks cranes. The replica of the Vulcan, the first iron boat built in Scotland is on the left. (Upper)

A sailing canoe on the Monkland canal at Summerlee. (Lower)

remarkable. Though the pace of physical expansion has slowed down, Summerlee, by judicious mixture of social and industrial history, spiced by special events to appeal to people of all ages, has become a real community museum, attracting well over 100,000 visitors a year. The mixture of indoor and outdoor facilities, the variety of items on display, the ever-changing spectacle of a developing museum, and an attractive, sheltered site all combine to make a deservedly popular attraction.

To make sense, in description, of a complex site is difficult, and the following account is not complete. It does, however, give something of the flavour of this remarkable museum.

ENTRANCE AND IMMEDIATE IMPACT

Summerlee is approached from the Cross at Coatbridge by West Canal Street, which crosses the route of a canal branch to Summerlee and Gartsherrie ironworks, and Heritage Way, at one time a private road leading to the Summerlee works. Beyond the former lodge, the entrance is marked by a punching and shearing machine, and by twin cast-iron columns (from a Glasgow railway bridge) carrying the name SUMMERLEE. Through the gate one can see the red and white brick main building, but it is probably the tram waiting on the left that first intrigues.

Of the three trams currently in service, two are Continental, but the third is a Lanarkshire Tramways Company vehicle being restored in the museum workshop. Putting off the delights of a tram trip for the time being one can turn right to Summerlee Cottages, a row of stone buildings which formerly stood on the other side of the approach road. On their new site these now house shops, the Ironworks Gallery, toilets and offices. Beyond the cottage, a path winds down the canal, past terraces on which are mounted heavy exhibits, including a gas purifier box from Newton Stewart, a Tropenas/Bessemer converter from a Hamilton steel foundry and machines from Hudson's Sheepford Boiler Works at the other end of Coatbridge. Eschewing the joys of the canal itself one can return to the main building, most conveniently entered through a low brick building relocated from the Lochrin Ironworks on the south side of Coatbridge. This now houses the museum tea room.

MAIN DISPLAY AREA

Through double doors the visitor can see, and hear what is marketed as 'Scotland's noisiest museum'. The engineering works setting is divided up by low partitions which allow the structure of the buildings to be seen. Immediately inside the entrance is a little gas engine, with, beyond, a shovel forge, representing a characteristic local industry.

Opposite, in a low shed, is a brass-finisher's shop with lathes and other tools. These are used by the museum's workshop staff to make and repair machine parts, which gives life to the shop. To the right of the entrance is a tinsmith's shop. To the right of this display area is a section used for small exhibitions, and beyond that is the iron and steel section. This has a large-scale model of part of the Summerlee Works which can be viewed from an elevated walkway against a background of a glazed screen wall with an industrial landscape beyond.

In the next bay is one of the Coatbridge-built steam colliery winding engines from Cardowan Colliery, near Glasgow. This is displayed as if being erected in an engineering works, with the parts named. The third bay is set out as the machine hall in a trade exhibition with a superb collection of machine tools, mainly by Scottish makers. Some of these operate, and together they give a fine impression both of an important manufacturing industry and of the tools used to make other machines. Beyond this are a workshop and storage bays, not open to the public.

EXCAVATED REMAINS OF IRONWORKS

Leaving the main display area on the glazed side, one can cross to the edge of the platform on which it is built and view the excavated remains of the Summerlee Ironworks. Though founded in 1836, the most conspicuous remains in front of the glazed screen are foundations of blast furnaces built in the 1890s. There are the jagged collapsed remains of the furnace hearths, surrounded by the concrete plinths on which stood the columns to support the furnace's structure. Under these can be traced the stone plinths for the 1836 furnaces. Also visible are drainage channels, flues for furnace gases, and the flat circular bases of stoves used to preheat air being blown into the furnaces. To the right a mass of brick and stonework can be deciphered as the remains of two houses for machinery to blow air into the furnaces with the settings for steam boilers and the base of chimneys, the whole giving a unique impression of the scale of one of the ironworks which were Coatbridge's most renowned industrial units.

Beyond the furnaces lies the canal, which can be reached by following the railings right towards the entrance and passing the machinery previously mentioned. The canal, re-excavated before the museum was created, is a section of the Gartsherrie and Summerlee branch of the Monkland Canal. As one follows the towpath to the left, one can see a basin, with the remains of tipping devices for loading coal into 'scows' as the barges on the canal were termed. Further along the towpath is a boatbuilder's shed, first erected at the Glasgow Garden Festival, and now used as a woodworking shop for the museum.

COAL MINE AND HOUSES

The most recent additions to Summerlee lie beyond the canal, and are grouped round the terminus of the tramway. These are a re-created coal mine, based on a small Lanarkshire drift mine, with simulated underground experience. Above ground, the Newcomen engine from Farme Colliery, Rutherglen, has been assembled with a mixture of old and new parts. Across the road are two ranges of miners' rows built to simulate how miners and their families would have lived at various periods since the establishment of Summerlee. At the pithead is a very effective re-creation of a coal-merchant's yard, and behind the pithead is a row of industrial locomotives, including the last steam locomotive to work in Lanarkshire, the last surviving Monklands-build locomotive, and a Sentinel steam shunter used in R.B. Tennent's rolling mill roll-making works in Coatbridge. Other large exhibits are displayed beside the main display building, and include two large steam cranes from Lanarkshire steelworks, including one unique 'three motor' (six cylinder) crane, and a South African Railways Beyer Garratt Locomotive on loan from Springburn Museum. The Garratt articulated locomotive was built in Glasgow by the North British Locomotive Company under sub- contract from Beyer Peacock of Manchester.

Summerlee not only caters for the industrial tourist. Displays in the main range feature social history, including wartime in Lanarkshire, and the Ironworks Gallery is an art gallery for Monklands District. Weekend events are held throughout the summer to appeal to a wide range of tastes.

TOLBOOTH MUSEUM, STONEHAVEN

The Harbour, Stonehaven, Aberdeenshire

Tel: c/o Arbuthnot Museum, Peterhead (01779) 477778

Open: *June to September, closed Tuesdays*

Admission: *Free*

Refreshments: *Nearby*

Parking: *Public car park nearby*

Disabled access: *One room not accessible, no toilet*

The museum is housed in the former tolbooth, which dates from the 16th century, and contains local history displays which include fishing and maritime items. There are also two unusual machines; one for making tobacco pipe lids, and the other for rope-making.

In the Market Square there is a plaque which reads 'THE BIRTHPLACE OF ROBERT WILLIAM THOMSON THE INVENTOR OF THE PNEUMATIC TYRE BORN 29TH JUNE 1822 DIED 8TH MARCH 1873'. This may confuse visitors who were under the impression that another Scotsman, John Boyd Dunlop, invented the pneumatic tyre. Thomson was an engineer and inventor who, later in life, became well-known for his steam-powered road vehicles, many of which were exported; sadly, none survive. At the age of 23 he patented two types of pneumatic tyre, one of which consisted of several tubes within one tyre. During a test in 1847 the tyres successfully covered 1,200 miles (1,930 km) but their high cost and some practical difficulties prevented their commercial success. A short section of Thomson's multi-tube tyre is preserved by the Royal Automobile Club in London. Dunlop patented his successful pneumatic tyre in 1888. Thomson is also commemorated in the local library where there is an 'R. W. Thomson Memorial Reading Room'.

TOMPHUBIL, LIMEKILN

Tomphubil, Near Tummel Bridge, Perthshire & Kinross

View from footpath

The enlightened policy of Perth and Kinross District Council in actively conserving industrial monuments is exemplified by their work on this isolated kiln, which is a landmark on the B846 road.

Tormiston Mill, Orkney, a good example of a late-Victorian watermill. In the 1960s it was converted into a restaurant and shop and is now operated as a visitor centre for the great Maes Howe chambered burial cairn.

It is an unusually large kiln for its location, and was presumably intended to supply agricultural lime to a significant area. Most of the numerous Perthshire kilns were small rubble-built structures serving very local needs.

TORMISTON MILL, ORKNEY

Stenness, Orkney
Tel: (0131) 244 3101

Open: *All year, daily*

Admission: *Charges*

Refreshments: *Restaurant*

Parking: *Good car and coach park*

Disabled access: *Limited*

This is a typical late-Victorian Orkney mill, on a rectangular plan, with a large cast-iron water wheel and spectacular stone-built lade. It was converted to a craft shop and restaurant in about 1970, and acquired, as a visitor centre for Maes Howe chambered burial cairn, by Historic Scotland in about 1990. Though the original interior has been obscured in the successive adaptations of the building, the stones and gearing remain, and the building is still worth visiting as a mill, apart from its other attractions.

TUGNET, ICE HOUSE

Speymouth, Moray
Tel: (01309) 673701

Open: *May to September, daily*

Admission: *Free*

Refreshments: *None*

Parking: *Limited*

Disabled access: *Good*

Commercial salmon fishing has been practised for many centuries on the rivers and along the coasts of Scotland. It is now in serious decline, for many reasons. Where there were significant runs of salmon, as at the mouths of major rivers, the fishing stations built by landowners could be large and elaborate. The finest such station in Scotland is probably Tugnet, at the mouth of the Spey, where fish were caught both with fixed nets and from boats. The court of houses, stores and boiling house is not open to the public, but the magnificent three-chamber vaulted ice house is, and contains a display on salmon fishing. The ice house was built in 1836 (not 1636 as suggested by a datestone above the entrance) and is the largest in Scotland.

The three-chambered vaulted ice house of 1836 at Tugnet salmon fishing station, Speymouth. It now houses displays on the history of salmon fishing.

UGIE SALMON FISH HOUSE, PETERHEAD

Peterhead, Aberdeenshire
Tel: (01779) 476209

The Ugie Salmon Fish House, with the 1585 wing on the right.

Open: *All year, daily, except Sunday*

Admission: *Free*

Refreshments: *None*

Parking: *Car park*

Disabled access: *Good*

This little building is the oldest in Scotland unequivocally linked to the fishing industry. The date of 1585 on the skewput of one of the gables has all the appearance of being in its original place, so that one wing of the building is more than 400 years old. It was built as a salmon-fishers' bothy, a type of structure still in use on the east coast of Scotland, where the ancient craft of fishing for salmon with nets is practised. This one is open to the public, and smoked and fresh salmon may be bought there.

UNICORN (HM FRIGATE)

Victoria Dock, Dundee City
Tel: (01382) 200900

Open: *All year*

Admission: *Charges*

Refreshments: *Hot drinks and snacks*

Parking: *Car park*

Disabled access: *Limited, no toilet*

HMS *Unicorn* was launched in 1824 at Chatham Dockyard on the Thames but, following the reduced requirement for warships after the Napoleonic Wars, she was never rigged. Before being laid up in reserve, a roof was built over the deck and

HM Frigate *Unicorn being moved in 1962. She is now moored in Victoria Dock, Dundee.*

this protective covering remains in position today. *Unicorn*, as designed, would have had three masts, carried 46 guns and been the equivalent of a modern cruiser. As a floating hulk she served as a gunpowder store at Woolwich Arsenal and then, in 1873, she was towed to Dundee and used as a Drill Ship. When no longer required by the Royal Navy, the Unicorn Preservation Society took over the ship in 1968 and by 1975 she was opened to the public during the summer months. Now, as the oldest British-built ship afloat, she is a popular attraction in Victoria Dock.

The fact that *Unicorn* was effectively 'mothballed' has resulted in her hull surviving remarkably intact whereas most wooden vessels in service needed extensive repairs and replacements. Here is a rare chance to study the construction of probably the best preserved old wooden hull in the world. It also represents the end of the era when wood and sail dominated warship design, because steam-engined ironclad warships took over in the mid 19th century. In the *Unicorn*, some reinforcing structural parts were made in iron, such as the 'knees' which join the underside of the deck beams to the sides of the ship; this use of iron reinforcment was introduced by Sir Robert Seppings in 1810 and further examples of his improvements can be seen in the bows and all along the lower hull where diagonal 'riders' made of iron are fitted.

The displays on board explain very clearly what life was really like in the Royal Navy during the early 19th century.

VERDANT WORKS, DUNDEE

27 West Henderson Wynd, Dundee City

Tel: (01382) 226659

Open: *June to August, Monday to Friday*

Admission: *Charges*

Refreshments: *Yes*

Parking: *On street*

Disabled access: *Limited*

Dundee has had a long and distinguished connection with the 'linen trade' (which includes the processing of jute), and had for many years both the largest jute, and the largest linen mill in the world. Most of the great jute and linen mills have either been demolished or converted to other purposes, mainly to housing, but it has long been the objective of some Dundee people to establish a textile museum. At various times that idea has seemed to be realisable, only for hopes to be dashed. Now Verdant Works, one of the smaller, and therefore more manageable mills has been acquired by Dundee Heritage and is being adapted as a museum, offices, and workplace. Verdant Works was founded as a flax-spinning mill in 1833, and was subsequently extended after a fire in 1852. It has a Gothic-detailed cast-iron framed attic comparable in quality, if not in scale, with those in the largest Dundee jute and flax mills, and has a fine unaltered office. Though not yet fully open to the public, Verdant Works is something well worth waiting for.

Verdant Works, Dundee, a small flax-spinning mill now being developed as a museum of Dundee industry.

WEST HIGHLAND MUSEUM

Cameron Square, Fort William,
Highland
Tel: (01397) 702169

Open: *All year Monday to Saturday; July & August,
Sunday (p.m.)*

Admission: *Charges*

Refreshments: *None*

Parking: *Car park*

Disabled access: *Inaccessible to wheelchairs*

The West Highland Museum is housed in the former British Linen Bank building which is not an ideal design for a museum with its small rooms and stairs. The museum is very much a museum of the West Highlands covering the colourful history of the area, armour and weapons, Highland dress, medals and Bonnie Prince Charlie relics.

Transport and industry are mentioned with small, but interesting displays. The oldest transport relic is a log-boat found in Loch Treig. A small exhibition tells the story of the Caledonian Canal built by Thomas Telford and opened, after many problems, in 1822. One of the major engineering feats illustrated is the series of locks, just north of Fort William, known as 'Neptune's Staircase'. Of course, the canal is still in use and can be inspected by visitors. The story of the West Highland Railway, built towards the end of the 19th century, is illustrated with photographs. But a road transport photograph tops them all – Henry Alexander drove a Ford Model T to the top of Ben Nevis in 1911, and descended safely.

Two relatively modern industrial projects which had limited success are described. There is an account of the aluminium smelting process carried out in the works at nearby Lochaber, and a model of the ill-fated paper pulp-mill of the 1960s which failed for a number of reasons, transport difficulties being one of them.

WICK HERITAGE CENTRE

20 Bank Row, Wick, Caithness, Highland
Tel: (01955) 605393

Open: *June to September (closed Sundays)*

Admission: *Charges*

Refreshments: *None*

Parking: *Public car park nearby*

Disabled access: *Inaccessible due to steps*

The Wick Heritage Centre is a very good example of what can be achieved by enthusiastic volunteers – and they have a number of awards to prove it, including the Museum of the Year Award for Scotland in 1982. The museum is housed in buildings which were part of the harbour area designed by the great Scottish engineer Thomas Telford, who also built the nearby bridge over the Water of Wick.

The displays feature reconstructed scenes, including several illustrating domestic interiors. Of the local industries, fishing was by far the most important as Wick produced almost half of the total herring exported from Scotland in the 1860s. In addition to fishing boat models, there are nets, various items of equipment used by the fishermen, and a machine for gutting fish. A large kiln for smoking herring to produce kippers has been renovated. At one time there were 50 companies making kippers in Wick. There is a very impressive harbour scene displaying boats and equipment from about 1850. The boats are all genuine and were built on the island of Stroma, which is just a few miles north of John o'Groats.

Fishing generated on-shore industries, such as fish-gutting. A figure of a girl doing this unpleasant task reveals the fact that she could clean about 35 fish per minute – for a whole day. Barrels were needed to transport fish and a display shows clearly how a barrel was made. At one time there were 650 coopers in Wick, but the industry died in the 1980s when plastic containers finally replaced barrels. There is also a complete blacksmith's shop and foundry.

The rescue services were very important in the stormy conditions around these northern coasts and they are featured with displays of life-saving equipment including rockets and a 'breeches buoy'. Lighthouses make an important contribution to safety at sea and the museum has on display the light and its clockwork mechanism from Noss Head Lighthouse 3 miles (5 km) north of Wick. This lighthouse was built by Alan Stevenson who also built the **Skerryvore Lighthouse.** The huge lens system and the lamp can be seen at one level, while on the floor below is the weight-driven clockwork mechanism which rotated the lens system to provide the flashing light.

Finally, the Wick Heritage Society are custodians of the Johnston Collection of photographs, taken by three generations of a local family between 1863 and 1977. About 70,000 negatives survive and these include many illustrations of industrial and transport subjects, fishing, farming, railways and early motor cars.

APPENDIX

ADDITIONAL RELATED COLLECTIONS

The following museums have small collections of industrial or transport related material:

BROUGHTY CASTLE MUSEUM
Broughty Ferry, Dundee
Maritime (see entry for **Dundee Art Gallery & Museum**)

BUCKIE MARITIME MUSEUM
Townhouse, West Cluny Place,
Buckie, Moray
Fishing

DALBEATTIE MUSEUM
Southwick Road, Dalbeattie,
Kirkcudbrightshire
Local history: quarries, mills,
maritime and railway

ERROL STATION RAILWAY HERITAGE CENTRE
Errol Station, Errol, Perthshire
Preserved station and local
railway history

EYEMOUTH MUSEUM
Auldkirk, Market Place,
Eyemouth, Berwickshire
Fishing

FALCONER MUSEUM, FORRES
Tolbooth Street, Forres,
Moray
Local history, bicycles

FOCHABERS FOLK MUSEUM
Pringle Antiques, High Street,
Fochabers, Moray
Horse-drawn vehicles

GEORGE WATERSON MEMORIAL CENTRE
Fair Isle, Shetland
Fishing, small boats and crofting

HALLIWELLS HOUSE MUSEUM, SELKIRK
Halliwells Close, Market Place,
Selkirk
Ironmongery

HUNTLY MUSEUMS
Drill Hall, Deveron Road,
Huntly, Aberdeenshire
Stonemason's yard, photography

LOSSIEMOUTH FISHERIES AND COMMUNITY MUSEUM
Pitgaveny Street, Lossiemouth,
Grampian
Fishing

MUSEUM NAN EILEAN
Town Hall, Stornoway,
Isle of Lewis
Maritime, fishing and agriculture

NAIRN FISHERTOWN MUSEUM
Laing Hall, King Street,
Nairn
Fishing

NEWHAVEN HERITAGE MUSEUM
Fishmarket, Newhaven Harbour,
Edinburgh
Local history and fishing

ROYAL NATIONAL LIFEBOAT INSTITUTION
West Quay Road, Poole,
Dorset
Lifeboat Stations and Museums
Guide (leaflet available)

SCALLOWAY MUSEUM, SHETLAND
Main Street, Scalloway,
Shetland
Maritime and fishing

SCOTTISH TELECOMMUNICATIONS MUSEUM
c/o British Telecommunications,
Pitsligo Road, Morningside,
Edinburgh
History of telephones
(undergoing relocation 1994)

SCOTTISH UNITED SERVICES MUSEUM
Hospital Square, The Castle,
Edinburgh
Models:ships and army vehicles

602 SQUADRON (CITY OF GLASGOW) MUSEUM
Queen Elizabeth Avenue,
Hillington Industrial Estate,
Glasgow
Aero engine and model aircraft

SKYE MUSEUM OF ISLAND LIFE
Kilmuir, Portree,
Isle of Skye
Blacksmith's shop, weaving
and crofting

TINGWALL AGRICULTURAL MUSEUM
Veensgarth, Gott,
Shetland
Crofting and horse-drawn
implements

TOMINTOUL VISITOR CENTRE
The Square, Tomintoul, Moray
Local history, peat-cutting and
cycles

The Stationery Office

Published by The Stationery Office and available from:

The Stationery Office Bookshops
71 Lothian Road, Edinburgh EH3 9AZ
(counter service only)
49 High Holborn, London WC1V 6HB
(counter service and fax orders only)
Fax 0171-831 1326
68-69 Bull Street, Birmingham B4 6AD
0121-236 9696 Fax 0121-236 9699
33 Wine Street, Bristol BS1 2BQ
0117-926 4306 Fax 0117-929 4515
9-21 Princess Street, Manchester M60 8AS
0161-834 7201 Fax 0161-833 0634
16 Arthur Street, Belfast BT1 4GD
01232 238451 Fax 01232 235401
The Stationery Office Oriel Bookshop
The Friary, Cardiff CF1 4AA
01222 395548 Fax 01222 384347

The Stationery Office publications are also available from:

The Publications Centre
(mail, telephone and fax orders only)
PO Box 276, London SW8 5DT
General enquiries 0171-873 0011
Telephone orders 0171-873 9090
Fax orders 0171-873 8200

Accredited Agents
(see Yellow Pages)

and through good booksellers

Printed in Scotland for The Stationery Office by CC No 3808 15c 7/97